EIGHTEEN HUNDRED MILES ON A BURMESE TAT

THROUGH BURMAH, SIAM AND THE EASTERN SHAN STATES

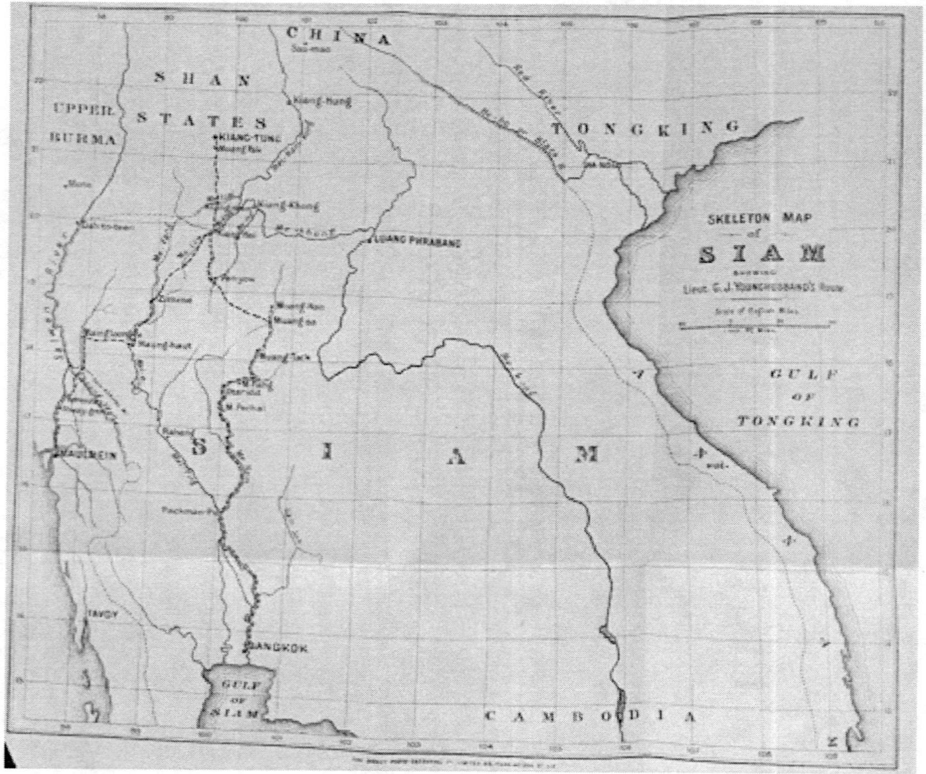
SKELETON MAP
of
SIAM
SHOWING
Lieut. G. J. YOUNGHUSBAND'S Route
CHINA
SHAN
STATES
UPPER
BURMA
KIANG-TUNG
LUANG PHRABANG
TONGKING
GULF
OF
TONGKING
SIAM
MAULMEIN
TAVOY
BANGKOK
GULF
OF
SIAM
CAMBODIA

EIGHTEEN HUNDRED MILES ON A BURMESE TAT

THROUGH BURMAH, SIAM AND THE EASTERN SHAN STATES

G. J. YOUNGHUSBAND

Published by

Facsimile Publisher
12 Pragati Market
Ashok Vihar, Ph-2
Delhi-110052
facsimilepublisher.com

Distribution Network
gyanbooks.com
India, USA, Canada, UK, Australia, France

ISBN : 978-93-5324-517-7 (HB)
First Published, London, 1888

2nd Impression 2020

Printed at: Gyan Press, Delhi.

Eighteen Hundred Miles on A Burmese Tat
Author: G. J. Younghusband

EIGHTEEN HUNDRED MILES
ON A BURMESE TAT

THROUGH BURMAH, SIAM, AND THE EASTERN SHAN STATES.

BY

AN ORDINARY BRITISH SUBALTERN,

TO WIT

LIEUTENANT G. J. YOUNGHUSBAND,

QUEEN'S OWN CORPS OF GUIDES.

LONDON:

W. H. ALLEN & CO., 13 WATERLOO PLACE,

PALL MALL, S.W.

1888.

PREFACE.

THE following pages give an account of a journey made during six months' leave in the beginning of 1887. They do not profess to any literary merit whatever, but are merely a faithful record of new countries and new nations, as seen with the eyes of an

ORDINARY BRITISH SUBALTERN.

CONTENTS.

EIGHTEEN HUNDRED MILES ON A BURMESE TAT.

CHAPTER I.

MOULMEIN TO ZIMMÉ.

Author obtains leave, and decides on travelling in Siam—Land journey begins at Moulmein—Travelling party—Moulmein to Shwaygoon—Detention at Shwaygoon—Elephants and their loads—My Burmese Tat—Teak logs floated down—Ananias armed—Plan for carrying rifle on horseback—Service tent discarded—Thoungyeen River, boundary Burmah and Siam—Wrong track taken—Ascend Taik Pyoung Mountain—Elephants unsuited to hill work—Elephant lifting timber—Mules or ponies for hilly country—Elephant howdah—Elephant skin not sensitive—Ananias changes apparel—Stockade at Mainloungye—Visit from Lord Chief Justice—Smoking cigarettes universal—Start for Muang Haut—Archbishop a failure.

HAVING obtained six months' leave, and being sick of the pomps and vanities of this civilized world of ours, I determined to take upon myself the cloak of an explorer, and to penetrate into a new country. I hoped to combine business with pleasure, to bring back many useful geographical and other facts, and also to get some good shooting in a virgin country.

Siam was the country chosen. Lying as it does side by side, throughout its length, with our new kingdom of Burmah, little known, and never thoroughly explored, it promised an interesting opening to the explorer and sportsman. Having settled on the country, it was determined to penetrate into it by land from British Burmah, as being more expeditious and likely to afford better sport, and not up one of the great rivers from the Gulf of Siam. However, I may as well anticipate so far as to say that we got no shooting worth speaking of throughout our long journey; the reader therefore who is on the look-out for a book on Sport in Siam, may knock off without taking the trouble to read any more.

Our land journey commenced at Moulmein in the Tenasserim Division of Southern Burmah, where we were most kindly and hospitably entertained by Colonel and Mrs. Plant. We were mere waifs and strays, utter strangers to the place and people, cruising around in rather a hopeless way in search of an hotel and dinner, when a good Samaritan in the genial person of Colonel Plant swooped down on us, in a miniature dog-cart, and carried us off to the pleasantest and most hospitable house in Asia. There we found Mrs. Plant and one or two friends, and our week at Moulmein slipped away so pleasantly and quickly, that I found myself seriously contemplating taking root there and sending in my application to be appointed Adjutant of the Moulmein Volunteers. However, all joys must have an end, and ours followed the general run of them. We started from Moulmein on Jan. 24th, 1887, and commenced our journey by steam launch up the Salween River.

Our party consisted of my orderly, a right, tight little Goorka from my regiment, named Judh Bir; a Madrassi cook boy, to whom his godfathers and godmothers had given the regal name of David at his baptism; but which I, not finding him up to a Hebraic monarch's form, changed to Ananias, as being a more characteristic name; my interpreter, who might have passed for anything from a ship's steward to the native Archbishop of Tahita, with a slight leaning towards the latter; and lastly myself. Ananias and I were strangers, but with the Archbishop I had a sort of bowing acquaintance, having seen him in the days of my youth in a wood engraving on the back of a missionary tract, amongst a group of other native Christians, all in tall hats and white chokers.

Our only four-footed companion was a small, iron-grey Burmah pony, standing just 12 hands 2 in. high, with the girth and legs of a galloway. A jolly, merry little fellow, but, as will be seen hereafter, quite childish in his love for inconvenient flippancy.

From Moulmein to Shwaygoon, a small village sixty-three miles up the Salween River, there is a daily line of steam launches, run by the Salween River Steam Navigation Co., good roomy boats 60 ft. long by 12 ft. broad, and decked throughout their length. We tumbled our pony and baggage into one of these, and being ourselves comfortably accommodated in the bows, started on our journey. It was kind and considerate of the skipper putting us so far for'ard, for the stench abaft, from the cargo of dried fish on board, was quite overpowering. I have never been in the main sewer of London Town, but I can make a fair guess at what it is like, and should think a cargo of Burmese dried fish could compare very favourably with it.

The day was bright and exhilarating, the country grew more and more wooded and picturesque as we proceeded, and our little boat bowled merrily along at the rate of eight miles an hour. We stopped three or four times to unload passengers, and to take in new cargoes of them, and after an eight-hour run reached Shwaygoon. Unfortunately I could not speak the language, and the Archbishop, my Burmese pocket dictionary, I am sure did not do me justice in my endeavours to make myself pleasant to the jolly Johnny Burmans and their crowds of wives.

Shwaygoon is a small village of 100 houses and some 800 inhabitants; it consists of two long streets running parallel to the left bank of the river, and about forty yards from it. There are five or six native shops, but they contain nothing but tobacco, fruit, and country vegetables. An enterprising Chinaman sells Bass's beer at twelve annas (one shilling) a bottle; the Burmans, he told me, drink it in preference even to their own vile concoctions. There is a post-office, and posts run to Papheen and Hlaingbue twice a week, besides a daily service to Moulmein by steam launch.

We were kept a day at Shwaygoon waiting for baggage elephants. In the morning I tried all round for game, but saw nothing. In the afternoon the police lent me a "dug-out" and paddled me up stream; we shot a few imperial and green pigeons. The former are magnificent birds, weighing as much as a plump Indian chicken; they have the beautiful sheen on their wings common to English carrier pigeons, and large ruby-coloured eyes. Their skin is very thick, and it wants a hard-hitting gun to bring them down. For the table they have to be skinned as well as feathered. Green pigeons of three kinds are common in these parts—the yellow-green, the rock-green, and the ordinary green. All of these are excellent eating. Fish of all sorts abound both in the rivers of Burmah and Siam.

Towards evening the elephants arrived from Hlaingbue, and next morning, 26th January, early, we started up the east bank of the Salween. The whole of our baggage was not more than two respectable mule loads, but we had the greatest to-do to prevail upon the mahouts (eleph*ent*-men the Archbishop calls them) to load it up. It made me positively weep to see a great brawny elephant looking quite injured at having to carry a load that one of our regimental mules would have smiled sarcastically at. Having started them off, I saddled up my little 12–2 charger and casually sauntered on to his back. Now having been a cavalry soldier for some years, and rather fancying myself as a decent rider, I had never viewed this small atom of horse-flesh otherwise than in the light of a means of conveyance when I was tired. However, he very soon knocked all that nonsense out of me; for he went off like a streak of lightning, stampeded the two elephants, who immediately devastated the village, and shed my goods and chattels on the roofs of houses and up high trees; he then galloped as hard as he could straight at a twelve-foot palisade. I thought he was going to try and jump it, and said my prayers accordingly, but he was no such fool; he stopped as dead as a mummy about three feet off it, and shot me violently into the hardest palisade ever made by man. He then stood quite still and sniggered at me. No other pony have I ever seen even smile, but that little rat distinctly grinned. I was rather wrathful and very much bruised; but mounted again, thinking that, having had his little joke, he would go along in a decent and decorous frame of mind. Not a bit; he went off harder than ever, this time through almost impenetrable forest, where he very shortly left me hanging over a bough like a night-shirt on a clothes' line. After that I led him till I got on to a good open bit of road, intending to have my joke there; but he wouldn't play at all then, and neither whip nor spur would stir him out of an old gentleman's tit-up. A tremendous wag that pony—I say it without malice—but in spite of my earnest endeavours to rival him in that respect, he invariably, throughout our long partnership of 1800 miles, managed to turn the tables on me, and make me the butt of all his little pleasantries. I named him "Joe" after a facetious donkey that used to delight Calcutta audiences at Wilson's circus.

Our road lay through dense level forest and high elephant grass, with a few Kareen villages dotted about in it. We halted the night at the Forester's hut at Kumawlay village, which lies about a mile off the river.

In the morning I went down to it, in the hopes of seeing a few ducks, but was disappointed; in fact we only saw one flight of ducks on the Salween River throughout its length—this in January. Opposite Kumawlay a bamboo or rattan boom has been laid across the river, to catch all logs floated down from the teak forests in the upper reaches of the river. Each log is marked with its owner's mark, and the forest officers, levying a small toll on each, pass them under the boom and allow them to float down to Moulmein.

As we were now getting into unsettled parts where bands of dacoits might be found on the prowl, I distributed arms to my small party. Judh Bir, my orderly, and the Archbishop, each had a Martini-Henry carbine, and I carried a double-barrelled shot gun. Ananias, the cook-boy, we securely lashed to a revolver; this was considered a necessary precaution, for he was in such a terrific funk of it that he would otherwise have hastened to hand it over, as a propitiatory offering to the first foe he happened to meet. Our experiences in Affghanistan had taught us this; there, owing to the howls set up by Exeter Hall people and other old women, the dhooly-bearers (ambulance carriers) who had previously gone unarmed were furnished with old condemned swords and sword bayonets; the natural result of which was, that when the dhooly-bearer happened to get caught by an Affghan, not only did he hand over a weapon to the enemy, but had the rather morbid gratification of being killed with it himself. Ananias's arguments in favour of not being armed were exceedingly sound. He contended that if he carried a revolver it might be looked on as an act of aggression on his part by the enemy, and that he might be mistaken for a soldier and made food for powder accordingly. However we compromised; he was to be allowed to conceal his revolver, and wear habitually his most lamb-like and conciliatory manner, on condition that he fired off all six chambers before running away in case of attack.

I have got a very good plan for carrying a rifle on horseback, from Gordon, 15th Hussars, who was Adjutant to Methuen's Horse at the Cape. It consists of a small leather bucket just big enough for the butt of the rifle, which is fastened to two D's on the off-side of the saddle, the rider holding the barrel in his right hand. This is certainly the best thing I have seen for mounted infantry.

Having settled these preliminaries, we moved on, with the Archbishop as an advance guard. All day the road lay through low forest-covered hills, and that night we put up in Thaidaw, a small Kareen village. The people were very kind to us, fed us with fowls and rice, and gave us a new bamboo hut to sleep in. Here, for the small sum of Rs. 3, we bought a very irregular-looking dog named Chieng-Zoung (ten fingers), the origin of whose name remains a dark mystery, on which his late master could throw no light. If anything, he favoured a greyhound, but there was also a strong dash of bull-terrier about him. He was coal black, and as hairless as a scalded pig. We had to carry him off in chains, much against his will, and did not set him free for several days for fear of his deserting us, and running back to his village. With a small party like ours it was imperative to have a watch-dog at night to take the place of a sentry. I have always found a dog a most effectual safeguard in many countries. A sentry may be caught napping, or circumvented, but a dog never; and certainly in that respect Chang (the name his high-sounding title degenerated into) upheld the canine reputation. His vigilance was quite overwhelming; he used to bark himself into a fit, and me into a foaming rage, at the slightest noise. He never took the least notice of any of us, and received any attempts at mild blandishments with silent contempt. However, he was a good dog and true, and we felt as if we had lost an old friend when we lost him within three days of our journey's end.

The next night we encamped in a wild wooded ravine on the banks of a small stream. At Colonel

Plant's recommendation, I had discarded my 80-lb. service tent, and instead of it had purchased a light shelter tent without poles, made of American drill. The idea was that at the end of a march we should all be too tired to pitch an 80-lb. tent, whereas the shelter tent could, with the aid of locally-cut bamboos, be rigged up in a few minutes. This shelter tent when pitched covered 20 ft. by 10 ft. of ground, and served admirably as a protection from the heavy dew for me and the whole of my party, but after a few days we found the labour of pitching it at night so great that we gave it up, and for the rest of our journey slept under thick trees, which we found quite sufficient to keep the dew off.

Our journey lay over a constant succession of densely-wooded hills for the next day and a half, when we reached the Thoungyeen River, the boundary between Burmah and Siam. Here there are two small ferry boats, and lower down stream a ford passable for elephants nearly all the year round. On the opposite bank there is a Siamese Guard Stockade, garrisoned by 13 old scarecrows, who call themselves soldiers. The toll usually charged is Rs. 2 per elephant and 2 annas per passenger, but they asked

Pony's Back hill

us for none. The old mummy who commanded the garrison asked us if we had seen or heard of any bands of dacoits; not that he had the slightest intention of sallying forth and wading in their gore, but rather with a view to making active preparations for a strong strategic movement to his right rear down the river. In the afternoon we headed up the Methawa River, a tributary of the Thoungyeen, meaning to take the Maingloungye road, but, owing to defective information, we got on to the wrong track. It was a day and a half before we discovered our mistake, being then within a few hundred feet of the summit of the Taik Pyoung Mountain. A passer-by told us of our error, and at first we sat around using indifferent language, but having fortified myself with stewed green parrot, I took a brighter view of life in general, and proceeded to scale the few remaining feet to the summit of the mountain. My reward was great, for the view was magnificent and very extensive. On the one hand the position of Moulmein was visible 100 miles S.E. as the crow flies, and on the other a lofty hill, which stands sentry over Zimmé on the far north; and on every side a countless succession of wooded hills. While on the subject of mountains I may mention that the aborigine, when he wants to make a track between two towns, chooses out the largest mountain anywhere within reasonable distance of his beat, and then proceeds to make his track in a bee line, straight over the highest peak of that mountain. Judh Bir and I often racked our brains and bored our fellow wayfarers to account for this, but without success. The fact remains however. In all these wooded hills grass for horses is very scarce, but we found that "Joe" took very readily to bamboo leaves, and throve on them; in fact he got quite aggressively fat in spite of the hard work.

We retraced our steps to within a few miles of the Siamese Guard Stockade, and there hit off the right track early on the second day. The marching onwards was very trying for all parties, alternately along the beds of bouldery streams and over steep hills. We often had to wade 200 and 300 yards in knee-deep water, encumbered with the hardest and most slippery boulders ever created. Poor old "Joe" seemed to suffer severely, having lost all his shoes; it was quite painful to see him try to pick his way along. I only discovered after I had walked 200 miles, out of compassion for him, that he was only pulling my leg, one of his little jokes at my expense.

Going down into the Me Grau Valley we had an opportunity of noticing the wonderful way in which an elephant gets down quite an apparently impossible-looking incline. He kneels down with his hind legs, and putting his fore legs straight out slides down those parts which are too steep to walk down. However, on the whole we came to the conclusion that an elephant is out of his element in the hills. He is born and bred in the plains, and there does work which both in quantity and quality is perfectly marvellous. Let any one who wants to see almost human intelligence in an animal go to the timber-yards of Moulmein, and there see the elephants at work manœuvring timber. I sat like a knot on a log for hours and watched them, and thought I had never seen anything so wonderful. What fascinated me more than anything was to see a tusker stacking timber, not six-inch planks, but great and mighty trees. As long as the stack was low enough for him to place the next log on it with his trunk, it was only wonderful; but when the stack grew higher, and to get the log up he had to rest one end of it on the top of the stack, and then with his foot just give the bottom end a kick which sent it up flying into its place, the wonderful became the marvellous. He seemed to do it as easily as you or I would kick a walking-stick on to the mantelpiece. This is not a yarn, as any one who knows Burmah can vouch for. It seems therefore a loss of power, intellectual and physical, to put a beast capable of such prodigies to carry a wretched mule-load up and down hill. In the hills his great intelligence brings him through difficulties which it is hardly fair to put to a beast of his huge ungainly bulk; he works under protest, and in a slow and laboured way. I should recommend a traveller rather to buy packed mules or ponies in Moulmein or Rangoon. These animals will cover their marches one-third sooner than an elephant, and carry very nearly as much, animal for animal. A Burmese elephant howdah must have been invented by the patron saint of elephants; it is 2 ft. broad, 2 ft. deep, and 6 ft. long; and into this coffin it is impossible to stuff more than about 360 lbs. of baggage. All baggage for elephant carriage should be made up in small parcels, for the elephants, being only half trained, will often not kneel down to be loaded, and consequently everything has to be handed up to the mahout, and placed in the howdah by him. Whilst on the subject of elephants, I should like to question the truth of a well-worn "Story Book" story, to the effect that "an elephant has a most sensitive skin and feels the smallest mosquito bite acutely." I think that yarn must have come from the mosquito when he was full of wine, and well "on the buck." My experience of elephants certainly tended to show that they have skins quite as hard and impervious to injury as the cover of an ordinary hair trunk.

Ananias the cook-boy about this period began to shed the lovely apparel wherein he was wont to win the smiles of the Burmese ladies in Moulmein, and donned a duster for a head-piece, and an ancient shirt as a body garment. Both he and my orderly tried a seat on top of the baggage elephants for one march; but the ride appeared to have no charms for them, the whole of their time being taken up in avoiding instant dissolution through being swept off from their high perch by the thick forest boughs through which the elephant forced his way. They did not repeat the experiment, but preferred walking. On the 12th day from Moulmein we arrived at Maingloungye, the first place of any importance reached in Siam. The greater part of the town is enclosed in an oval stockade some 700 paces long and 400 paces broad. My orderly, who is a bit of a military critic, expressed huge contempt for this form of fortification; he considered that the only useful service which it performed was to keep the poultry of the inhabitants from straying. There was certainly some justification for this verdict, for the stockade was 12 ft. high, and by no possible means could the defenders fire either over or through it. We found the chief away, but his proxy was very kind to us, and gave us the court house to live in—an edifice not much used, from the look of it. After breakfast I noticed the Lord Chief Justice sitting on his hams outside, evidently sincerely gratified that the palace of justice was at last of service to some one. The chief's *locum tenens* visited me twice—a merry old gentleman without any clothes on worth mentioning. He was like a venerable child, and crowed with delight over my guns and toilet requisites, the sponge especially exciting great admiration. I gave him a glass of whiskey and a cigar, and though he pretended not to like the former, yet in the course of the day he brought all his relations, to the fifth generation, to have one too.

Men, women, and children smoke huge cigarettes about six inches long and one inch thick, contin-

The Chief of Chamtong one of the ugliest old gentleman I have ever seen. He must be a very wealthy man judging from the extent of his cultivated land and the very elegant hat he wears.

One of my Coolies.

to face p.18.

uously throughout the day, from dawn to dewy eve. Tobacco is very cheap and good, the usual price being 2 annas (threepence) for 1½ lbs. Cigar and cigarette cases being unknown, the inhabitants wear one of these colossal cigarettes in the lobe of each ear, and one in their mouths. I was horribly pestered with people who came to stare at me.

Next day we hired new elephants and set off for Muang Haut. The path lay through wooded, hilly country as before, and in the evening we bivouacked in a wooded glen on the banks of a stream. The Archbishop (my Archbishop) had turned out a hopeless failure as an interpreter, so I used to make him collect firewood, an occupation which made his haughty Eurasian blood boil with indignation. The way he did this job gives a good general idea of his character and manner of doing things. Having collected his wood at the summit of a little rise above the camp, he would proceed to throw it down, stick by stick, ten yards at a time, towards the camp fire. In this way he managed to take an hour over a job which he could have done in ten minutes if he had carried the bundle down. So in other things. I loved my Archbishop dearly, and paid him at the rate of Rs. 300 a month to gather sticks;

but, all the same, I determined that we must part as soon as opportunity offered.

We passed several large bullock caravans and trains of coolies carrying tea and poultry. These all travelled pretty close together for mutual protection, and had guards of eight or ten men each. They were armed with tower-marked muskets and "dahs." We also passed a Siamese military guard in charge of some bigwig, and six or seven elephants. They wore grey and white striped shirts, yellow belts, and dark blue skirts, their baggage being carried by every fifth man on a banghy pole, as shown in the picture.

The next night we encamped on the Me Lie River, in a pretty little basin surrounded by hills. I found out, by accident, that the pernicious Ananias had given my orderly no meat for two days, and the good little man, thinking I was tight for food, said nothing, but trudged his weary marches on dry rice. Having first smitten Ananias hip and thigh, I sent off Judh Bir to sit on the track to try and buy a fowl from some passing caravan. He soon came back immensely pleased with himself, hugging a huge and venerable cock, which it still makes my teeth ache to think of. On this day I solved the dark and deep mystery of my Archbishop's real calling and position in life. He was a volunteer in a distinguished corps. Now we all know, on the very best authority, that "one volunteer is equal to ten pressed men," and consequently my mind is lost in a hopeless whirlwind of conjecture as to the possible state of those ten men who go to make up my Archbishop.

CHAPTER II.

MOULMEIN TO ZIMMÉ—*continued.*

Muang Haut, on Me Ping River—Novel way of catching small fish—Tokhan elephant men desert—Proceed to Zimmé; coolies for baggage—Effect of civilization on semi-barbarous nations—Caravan Shan ponies—Advantage of a Doctor as explorer—Batong: cure of Chief's wife—Zimmé—Search for English residents—Dr. Cheek—Visit to the Prince's eldest son—King Theebaw—Incredulity regarding his Dethronement—A Prince increases his income—Visit to Siamese Commissioner—Carriages unprocurable; join Yunnan caravan—Difficulties in starting for Kiang Tung—Mysterious warning.

ON the 5th day from Maingloungye we reached Muang Haut, on the Me Ping River, one of the great rivers of Siam.* We halted here one day, and enjoyed the rest immensely, lolling about and watching the habits and customs of a new race.

* It may be well to note that "Ban" is the designation of small places in these parts, *i.e.* of from five to twenty houses, answering to our "village." Large places of from thirty to forty houses and upwards are called "Muang" or "Town," as for instance "Muang Haut," "Muang Nan." The largest places have no prefix, as for instance, "Zimmé," "Lacong."

LOOKING UP THE ME PING RIVER FROM MAUNG HAUT.

to face p. 22.

Awfully nice people we thought them, the women so clean, and plump, and pretty, and the men civil and obliging. We put up in the public rest house, and all the travellers who were in it very kindly turned out to make room for us. For this civility I was indebted to the fact that I had two elephants with me, an elephant apparently being a sign of rank and importance in Siam. Indeed, in describing a man of wealth, they invariably mention the number of elephants he possesses. Later on, when travelling with pack mules, I found that, though I was kindly treated, yet it was more like an equal.

The river is here about 150 yards broad, and is navigable for the ordinary country boats down to Bangkok and the sea on one hand, and up to Zimmé on the other; a magnificent stream, draining the kingdom of Siam from its northern borders to the Gulf of Siam. We saw at Muang Haut, to us, a very novel way of catching small fish. It was on the principle of the dynamite cartridge with which poachers at home make their hauls. Having enclosed a small piece of the river, about 30 yards long and 10 yards broad, two or three women wade about in it, hammering small hollow bamboo piles into the bed of it; the vibration apparently stupefies all the small fish, and they may be seen lying about stunned on the surface of the water, or else wildly jumping out on to the banks. Small children run about and pick them up. Next day we started north, heading up the river valley towards Zimmé, and everything went swimmingly till we reached Tokhan, a village about 20 miles short of that place. Here the elephant men put our baggage down, and walked off, leaving us stranded without any means of transport. Luckily the next day an artisan of Dr. Cheek's happened to pass that way, and I gave him a letter to take on to Zimmé asking for the loan of elephants to bring us in. Meanwhile we sat tight, and waited. Life in a Siamese village, more especially if it is out of the beat of former travellers, is quite unbearable to a European, by reason of the immense crowd which mobs him night and day. We always therefore tried to halt away from villages, as long as supplies and water were procurable. The night before we reached Tokhan we came on a solitary wayside hut, and found the inhabitants most kind and hospitable. Madame my hostess, a comely buxom damsel, assisted at my toilet, down to the smallest and most embarrassing details; and set covetous eyes first on all my cleaning

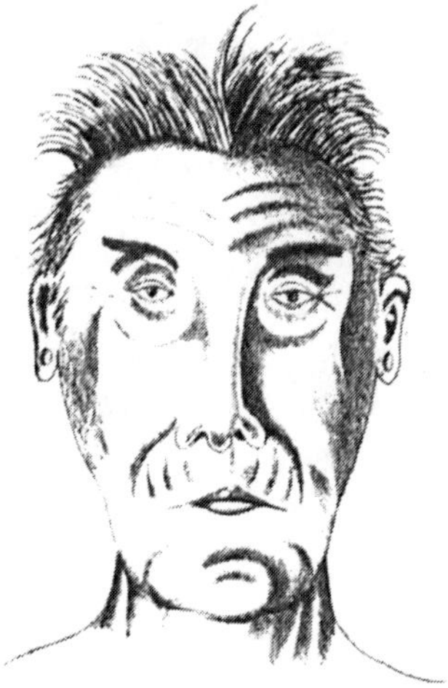

he Chief of Tokhan also the Possessor of a European
at but he rather hid his under a bushel whereas
ur friend of Chamtong doted on his, never parting
rom it for a moment.

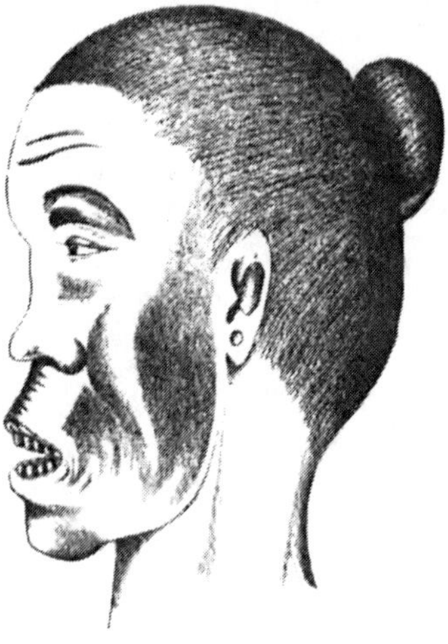

The Chief of Tokhan's head wife and a jolly merry life she leads the younger ones.

to face p. 24.

apparati in detail, and finally on myself. However, I said that I could not give her myself, as I had a wife at home (horrid fib!), and presented her with a cake of Pears' Soap as a peace-offering. She brought me a royal fowl in return. In Tokhan, or any other big village, life was a burden to me: the people mobbed me from dawn till late at night; and my meals were as good as a play to the majority of them. They would come and take pews all round me, about ten deep, and watch in solemn silence every mouthful I took. Very well meaning they were, and good natured, but a maddening nuisance. Though my temper is of a sweetness almost bordering on the idiotic, yet I would have given much for a few frenzied moments, with a big stick in my hand, in the midst of the throng that surrounded me. The chief was much encumbered with wives; but, as will be seen from the accompanying sketch, he had a very efficient first-lieutenant to keep them in order. I was living in a small house at the corner of his compound, and little knots of his wives used to come across to gossip; but the eagle eye of the first-lieutenant used very soon to spot them, and a shrill commanding voice sent them flying back to their work at the loom or the wheat-mill.

After waiting two or three days at Tokhan, and getting no answer or elephants from Zimmé, we determined to push on, the villagers promising to carry our things as far as the next village. It will be remembered that it made me weep to see what was considered an elephant load in these countries; imagine then my emotion at seeing what a man's load was. They fell on my modest packs and distributed their contents amongst about half of the adults of the village. Apparently a pair of boots and a silk pocket handkerchief, securely lashed to a stout bamboo banghy pole, is the average load for a man of Siam. I was full of wrath at the time, thinking that this was an artful device for putting four annas into the pockets of as large a crowd as possible; but when at the end of the stage I found that they had all come out of good fellowship, and not from hope of gain, and that they were all quietly walking off to their homes without asking for or expecting anything, my conscience smote me for my ingratitude, and a man was sent running after them with money to buy enough tobacco to make them all sick for a week.

These little incidents, as characteristic of a semi-barbarous nation, make one think of the effect of

One of our Elephant Drivers

A Laos of Muang Haut.

Boat on the Me Ping River

A Dingy or "dug out" on the Me Ping River

ace p. 27.

a highly-civilized government on the Oriental character with somewhat mixed feelings. Catch the gentle Hindu, who basks under the British Raj's brightest sun, doing anything for nothing! Not he; we get work out of him in three ways—firstly, by paying for it; secondly, by holding out hopes of gain in other ways—appointments, promotions, and such like; and thirdly, and mostly, by fear. Nothing do we get for love, and deuced little for a halfpenny.

Our way for the twenty odd miles into Zimmé lay through a level, richly-cultivated plain, watered by the Me Ping River, and thickly sprinkled with the pretty picturesque villages of the country. We passed a caravan of about eighty Shan ponies (generally known as Burmah ponies), hardy, thick-set little fellows, without any mouth to speak of, and not having a saddle pace in their compositions. Their draught power is, however, enormous; one sees them in Rangoon worrying along a great carriage at a most surprising pace. It is a pity something cannot be done to improve the breed for military purposes. They have tremendous strength, endurance, and staying power, and thrive on the scantiest fodder; all they want is size, and a longer rein. On this subject more anon, when we reach the Shan breeding-grounds.

The Siamese are certainly not an equestrian nation; so far, we had only seen one wretched little rat of a pony, resident in the country, and he picked up a precarious living in the ditches and drains, alongside the pariah dogs. All the great people ride on elephants, and the rest use their own legs.

It often occurred to us what great advantages a doctor would have over ordinary explorers in penetrating into wild and dangerous countries. A practising doctor might go with impunity into places which others could only enter with the gravest risk. An instance of abiding faith, of several horse-power, came under our notice in Batong, a village passed during the day. On our arrival we found the chief's wife down with a bad go of fever, and the chief, after receiving us, returned to a corner of the hut, and continued writing a long letter on strips of bamboo (in this country used instead of paper). After a bit I asked him what he was doing. "Writing a letter to the deity, asking for my wife to be cured." Madam, from the mattress, hearing my question, asked me to add a small postscript, backing up the chief's request. To humour the lady, I wrote

A superior description of house generally occupied by the Chief of a Village.

The Chief of San Batong father of the Cherub; has scrubby whiskers of which he is very proud

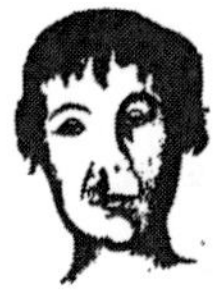

"A Cherub" whom the Printer and I have made conspicuously ugly.

to face p. 29.

my name and the date in English at the end of the letter, and then asked the patient how she felt. "Very much better!"—in fact, she immediately sat up, and sent for the betel box and tobacco tray. All sorts of people used to come to us to be cured of all kinds of impossible diseases and malformations. One father was greatly annoyed because we could not clap a pair of hands on to a child born without any. The chief of Batong told me, with becoming pride, that his family was thirty strong, all in and about the house. Amongst them were two very comely girls, and a very pretty child, whom I have managed to make conspicuously ugly in my sketch.

A short march of eight and three-quarter miles brought us into Chiengmai (in Burmese, Zimmé). The road lay through endless paddy fields, with small groves and bamboo clumps sprinkled about.

Zimmé is composed of two stockades; they contain about 8000 inhabitants; a long street of shops runs through them, the houses as you proceed getting thicker and closer, and the trees fewer. The shops are low shanties open to the streets, and contain chiefly prints and cheap cotton goods.

The market is held every morning, when the country people come in large numbers and establish themselves on the ground along each side of the main street.

These people sell all the daily necessaries of the Laos: betel, tobacco, eggs, dried fish, and lime pills—not a very wholesome diet, one would think, but the people chew betel to such an extent that I imagine they have little appetite left for food.

There is a wooden bridge about 300 feet long spanning the River Me Ping.

I rode into Zimmé alone, ahead of our party, knowing that a British Vice-Consul and several American missionaries were stationed there, and thinking that I should have no difficulty in finding them. After spending a couple of hours searching for them, I thoroughly lost myself, and, dismounting, stood in the market-place, surrounded by a gaping crowd of the inhabitants, and waited for some kind soul to take compassion on me, and show me the road. This a small boy did towards evening. I first visited Dr. McGilvery, an American doctor missionary, and one of the oldest resident foreigners in Siam. He gave me much useful information about the country and its people, and then passed me on to Dr. Cheek, a first-class fellow, to whom I owe many things besides thanks, as will be seen hereafter. I took the liberty of putting up at the Vice-Consulate, though its owner, Mr. Archer, was away on tour. My baggage, with the Archbishop, and my faithful orderly, arrived just before dark, and we spent a very comfortable night between four walls, for the first time since our journey began. Next morning I shot the sun, and fooled around with "meridian altitudes" and such-like scientific terms; and then went with Dr. Cheek to visit the Prince's eldest son, the Prince himself being away at Bangkok, handing over his only daughter to be one of the king's eight hundred wives. Eight hundred wives! doesn't it sound appalling? Personally, I have always found one quite sufficient; that is why I travel so much! I find I get on with Angelina much better by letter than any other way.* I found it quite true, when I visited Bangkok some months later, the king really had eight hundred and one wives; but when he goes away on three days' leave he only takes about two hundred of them with him. This is a solid-graven-image fact, for I saw one of his country houses a few miles from Bangkok, and it only had accommodation for two hundred wives!

* *Note to Publisher.*—If my wife orders a copy of this book please expunge the preceding few lines.

Poor fellow, how desolate he must feel, and cold at night, when such a large portion of his better half is far, far away! However, we are straying from our subject, viz. the Prince's son. He received us very affably, and I had a long conversation with him through Dr. Cheek. Amongst other things he asked whether the English really had taken Mandalay—this a year and a half after its actual occupation by the British. Dr. Cheek told me afterwards that for many months the Laos and Siamese scoffed at the news that the great and powerful monarch, King Theebaw, had fallen into the hands of the British, and even after the constant repetition of the news by travellers passing through they reluctantly accepted the fact, but only on the grounds that the English must have used magic to compass their nefarious ends. The Prince's son next asked what we had done with King Theebaw, and seemed greatly surprised that he had not been gently eased off into Paradise with thumbscrews, boiling oil, and other lingering comforts. And when I added that he and all his surviving wives were comfortably settled in Madras, with an ample income, he began to think that to be conquered by the British was rather a desirable culmination to one's career than otherwise.

I am sure that most princes in Siam would be only too delighted to get the same income as they do now as prisoners of war, and thereby be saved the trouble of screwing their salaries out of the pockets of their subjects.

One of the numerous ways in which the screw is applied came under our notice at Zimmé. During the floods in the previous year a large portion of the wooden bridge which spans the Me Ping River at this point was washed away, and one of the Princes was entrusted with the task of having it repaired. Our Royal Highness, instead of seeing anything derogatory to his birth and calling in doing this job, at once perceived an opening for making a little pocket-money, and accepted the duty with alacrity. Don't please suppose that his Royal Highness meant to cheat in a vulgar way over contracts and such like; that he left to lower mortals. No, he was a cut above that; his mode of making money was as follows. Having first built a comfortable little bamboo hut for himself near the scene of his future labours, he sent off his myrmidons to all the surrounding villages to collect labourers, every village being obliged to supply free labour for any government works in hand. Having collected a goodly number, our Prince sat tight and did nothing for two or three months. He then suddenly ordered a muster parade, and of course found that the majority of the labourers, thinking their services were not immediately required, had gone to their own homes. This was all his Royal Highness had been waiting for, and he immediately sent round and fined all the absentees heavily, thereby making a good lump sum for his own private expenditure. Mending bridges is evidently, from this example, a very paying business in Siam. When I passed through Zimmé, the above-mentioned illustrious person had managed to make a very handsome income out of the job, for the space of ten months, without even commencing the work of repair.

Our next visit was to the Siamese Commissioner, an official holding much the position of a British Resident at the Court of an independent Prince in India. He was quite superior to the Prince in civilization; he had tables, and chairs, and Havana cigars, and a visiting card printed in English, Colonel Something - very - long - and - unpronounceable. We were received with great kindness and courtesy, but not even Dr. Cheek's assurances would persuade him that I was not up to some devilment, such as annexing the country or introducing celibacy. One of his followers had been to Calcutta, and spoke with great admiration of the English and their city, at the same time adding, that if I wanted to see something considerable shakes better, I should go to Bangkok. The Commissioner very kindly gave me notes to the head men of villages, ordering them to supply me with food on payment: these I found most useful on one or two occasions.

Finding it hopeless to engage baggage elephants, or to buy suitable mules or ponies, we managed, through Dr. Cheek's kind endeavours, to attach ourselves to a caravan of Yunnan merchants on their way to Kiang Tung, the capital of the Trans-Salween Shan State of the same name. We were to start early next morning, and I set about getting my things ready. I had intended all along dismissing my Archbishop, who was thoroughly inefficient as an interpreter, and taking on any one I could pick up at Zimmé. Having prepared a parting speech of much severity, I sent for the Archbishop, with the kindly intention of pounding him with it, in the hopes of his giving up preying on the public in the light of an interpreter. However, he appeared so speechlessly drunk that he could not understand what I said; I paid him his wages therefore, and let him go—Rs. 200 (nearly £20) for three weeks' work!

Everything and everybody except Dr. Cheek seemed dead against our getting on further north. The Archbishop and a drunken boon companion of his, whose name I have forgotten, I am sorry to say, set to work to frighten my small retinue. My cook-boy came to me, pea green with funk and weeping bitterly, to say that he was told he was going to a place where the tenderest parts of his person would be immediately made into curry and rice; but that he was quite willing (this very ruefully) to die with master. And even my little Goorka orderly came with rather desponding stories about the dangers of the undertaking, and seemed quite to have made up his mind that he would never see his home again. The interpreter I had engaged, vice the Archbishop, was frightened by that worthy's boon companion into deserting me at the last moment, and I could get no other. Towards evening a native brought me a mysterious note scribbled in pencil, to the effect that my life was in danger, and that if I would follow the bearer, the writer would forewarn me of the deadly plot, so that I might be "on garde" (as the gentleman expressed it). Tying myself to a revolver,

I thought I might as well see if anything was up, and followed the servant. He led me to a general store shop, kept by an English man of sorts, who, after apologizing to me for not coming to me instead of sending for me, proceeded to unfold a blood-curdling tale of rapine and murder, in which it was intended I should play the most uncomfortable part. A party of Shans from Mokmay were dogging our steps, and were waiting only for a chance of pouncing upon us, that one of them had been making inquiries in the town concerning our firearms, what money or merchandise we carried, and so on. All these worries and anxieties, coming one on top of another, rather badgered one; it seemed as if the fates were dead against us. But the crowning misfortune came in the morning, when I found that the whole of my saddlery, down to the watering bridle, had been stolen in the night. This was very nearly the last straw, but after swearing to myself a bit in a corner, I felt better, and was just starting off on a blanket, with a rope bit, when my local guardian angel, in the shape of Dr. Cheek, turned up, and on hearing of my loss immediately insisted on presenting me with a whole brand new set of American saddlery. One can hardly realise the magnificence of this gift, till one gets a few thousand miles away from where saddles are made. Then Mrs. Cheek, after giving me a regular square meal, loaded me up with vegetables, fruit, and two most welcome bottles of curry powder; and with the hearty good wishes of both, I trotted off to meet my caravan, thirteen miles out. With me Dr. Cheek sent a native of Zimmé, to whom he explained who we were and where we were going, and instructed him to help us in getting food at the villages we passed.

The Chief and Leader of the Yunnan Caravan I travelled with.

My own sweet self after leaving Zimmé

My Zimmé servant

A Laos of Papao wh nearly boned one of our rifles.

to face p. 39.

CHAPTER III.

ZIMMÉ TO KIANG TUNG.

Leave Zimmé with Yunnan traders—Starting the caravan—Superstition—The pony's pranks—Kiang Hai on Me Khok River—Shans' physique and dress—Muang Loung—Approach Kiang Tung—Possible fatal ending of journey.

On February 20th we left Zimmé with a party of Yunnan traders *en route* to Kiang Tung. I changed a 1000 Rs. note into gold leaf, the only feasible means of carrying money.

Finding elephants a very broken reed to lean upon, I tried to buy mules from these traders, but as we could not come to terms I represented myself in need of carriage for about 300 lbs of merchandise for Kiang Tung. They agreed to carry it at 2 Rs. per diem, which suited me excellently.

Before dawn shrill calls are heard, and the ponies and mules, which have been out grazing all night, come trotting in. Sometimes one or two are missing, their owners show wonderful skill in tracking them out. The loads are all made up on the ground on a sort of trestle, and the pack is lifted bodily on to the saddle, which it fits exactly. The whole lot, fifty or more, are loaded in about five minutes. The leader of the caravan moves off on his pony, all the others follow in a string as they are loaded. The first day, much to my surprise, they got the whole caravan off before I had saddled my pony. Two or three of the mules are covered with bells, they move at a good three miles over any country and carry as much as 200 lbs. a piece.

The mules are small as a rule, the ponies are the regular Shan pony, known as the Burmah pony.

Starting at dawn they march about three hours and stop at the best grazing ground about that time. As each pony arrives, his pack is off in a second, his gear in two more, and then he gets a kick on the ribs and goes off to graze. After a halt of about two to three hours a gong is sounded to recall stragglers; the ponies and mules being called in as before, the caravan is off again in five minutes. At the halts the packs are neatly laid in rows and the men sleep at the ends enfilading them. One or two nights in dangerous places they threw out pickets up and down the road. On the road all the mules and ponies are muzzled to prevent delay from their grazing; they run along loose without any leading rope.

The Yunnans are fine healthy fellows, all walking except the bosses; five of them were armed with guns. I found that they stood in mortal dread of having their pictures taken: this was a happy discovery, for whenever they bother me I whip out my note-book and begin sketching one of them. The effect is instantaneous.

They are very superstitious, and we nearly had a serious misunderstanding because my boy grilled a fowl. This in their eyes is desperately wicked, and bound to incur the displeasure of the spirits. Consequently, after nearly frightening the boy to death, they set to work and fired off their guns, lit large fires, and took other precautions to keep off the evil one. Luckily nothing happened that night, for if a mule had strayed or anything gone wrong, it would have been put down to me and my fowl. I ate nothing but stews after this, and they were satisfied.

That pony of mine is quite the wickedest pony in Asia. He is only 12-2, but within that small compass is contained all the mischievousness of fifty children.

With much toil my boy gets me a basin of water to wash with; while I turn round to take off my coat, darned if that pony does not cruise round in a casual way and drink it, not because he is thirsty, for he has just had his bellyful of water.

I had a venerable solar topee, which I was keeping together with great trouble, when that pony, knowing it, deliberately eats the crown out.

Is my dinner cooking on the fire? Off he goes and tips it over.

Am I dead tired and fast asleep? He sticks his nose into me.

Do I want to give him his grain? He goes and stands on the far side of a quagmire, though he is dying to get at it.

Have I just been on the point of getting an angle with the prismatic? Up he comes, jogging my elbow. Have I tied him up with everything I possess? He eludes it somehow, slips his head-stall or breaks it so I have to let him loose.

When I am in a hurry to start, he hides behind a tree; when I want to go slow, he runs away; when I want to go fast, he pretends to be lame. Do I put

A fisherman at Kiang Hai

Two Kareens met beyond Kiang Hai

to face p. 43.

my watch or other treasures on the table? He waits till I look the other way, and then tips it over.

Seven days' march brought us to Kiang Hai, a fortified place on the Me Khok River. The place is in an extensive plain, with distant hills visible north and west. The houses are very thinly scattered amongst trees, and the population must be small for the size of the place.

The river is fordable for mules, though much larger than the Me Ping at Zimmé.

There are no shops at Kiang Hai, only a daily market held at the cross roads in the middle of the town, all the women squatting on mats along the side of the road, each with their little pile of goods.

Only fish, betel, tobacco, and the like are sold: no butchers here as at Zimmé (where there were many selling beef and pork). This is a dead-and-alive place, which might be of importance if it bestirred itself, situated as it is on a fine waterway, and also on the mainland routes from Burmah or China, surrounded by well-watered land.

The Me Khok River is the boundary between Burmah and Siam, but the Siamese have quietly encroached, and are ready to claim the country as far north as Me Tsai, making the boundary Kiangtsen.

The Me Khok is navigable for boats to the Me Kong River at Kiangtsen. This appears to be the main trade route between Moulmein and Luang Probang.

In the hills between Zimmé and Kiang Hai the nights were very cold and the days hot. The dew at night is very heavy. There are very few mosquitoes or sand flies at this season of the year.

The Shans are a hardier and more manly race than the Laos, though in physique they are not in any way superior. Compared with the hill-men on the N.W. frontier of India, they are nowhere, either in physique or martial bearing, Very few carry arms, and fewer still firearms. The men wear their hair long and tied in a knot on the side of the head, round the knot winding a small puggri during the day. Over this they wear a very broad-brimmed straw or bamboo hat, affording much shade and some protection from the sun. The women wear a turban, generally red, a short jacket, and the ordinary dhoty, but of brighter colour than the Laos. They are not so clean-looking, though they bathe constantly, and their houses are dirty.

I left Kiang Hai 27th Feb., passed Hai Tuk on the 4th March. On the 5th we followed the course of the Me Hai River, and after crossing the Noai Chang Mountains, from which we got no view on account of the mist, we reached the village of Muang Pak on the 6th March.

Nineteen miles brought us to Muang Loung, a few miles from Kiang Tung. I approached this place with rather mixed feelings. Would it be a short shrift and a bowstring, or a dress of honour and a welcome? However, it will be all the same a hundred years hence. From the country people I have seen I should not think there was any animosity against the English, and two parties of Shan carriers, who accompanied us all along, had been most friendly. We had come so fast that it would be difficult for any news of me to have gone before. Four miles over gently undulating bare downs brought us into Kiang Tung.

CHAPTER IV.

THE TRANS-SALWEEN SHAN STATE OF KIANG TUNG.

The Trans-Salween Shan State of Kiang Tung—Murder of Prince's sister by King Theebaw, and diminution of Burmese influence—Encroachments of Chinese and Siamese—Boundaries, and indifference of people to them—People of Kiang Tung repudiate encroachments, but do not resist—French and English possessions contiguous—Discuss policy—Government of the Province—Preponderance of women—Description of women—Dress of men—Easy way to procure a wife—Martial qualities of Shans—Make acquaintance with a Burman—Call on Prince's uncle—Visit to Prince—Servant of Margary—Judh Bir's good qualities—Yunnan pack-saddle—Manner of loading mules and ponies—Yunnan system of marching—Bullock caravans—Elephants as pack-animals—Shans fear Chinese; not on friendly terms with Laos—Ignorance of European politics—Kiang Tung on friendly terms with Shan State of Moné—Trade—Shans trade in ponies—No local coinage—Game—Kareen hunters.

KIANG TUNG is a large semi-independent Shan State which lies to the east of the Salween river.

It is, or rather was, nominally tributary to the King of Burmah; and tribute, in the shape of ivory,

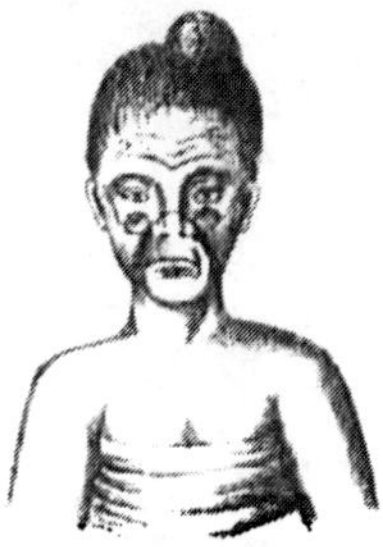

An old lady who lived opposite me at Kiang Tung

A child at Kiang Tung

A Kakow hill woman

A young lady of Kiang Tung

to face p. 46.

gold, and ponies, was yearly sent, until the massacre of the Kiang Tung Prince's sister a few years ago (1879 most probably) by King Theebaw. In retaliation for this outrage the whole of the Burmese Embassy then resident at Kiang Tung, the capital, were murdered, and diplomatic relations with the Court of Mandalay were broken off.

Although at the time King Theebaw vowed vengeance, and threatened an invasion, with the double intent of punishing the Kiang Tung Shans for their treachery, and of re-instating a Burmese Embassy, and Burmese influence in that State, yet his threats were never executed, and as far as Burmah was concerned Kiang Tung became practically an independent State.

Years of apathy or timidity have considerably reduced the size of the Province; the Siamese from the south and the Chinese from the north have both encroached to a considerable extent, and have taken possession undisturbed, and almost without protest, of large and valuable tracts of country.

The Chinese encroachment, from what information I could collect, aggregated more than 1000 square miles of country. But perhaps this statement should be received with caution, for my informants being

Yunnan merchants, and therefore naturally having a Chinese bias, would be inclined to magnify the Chinese acquisitions to the detriment of the Shans, whom they cordially hate.

From the Shans themselves I could extract no information with regard to their northern boundaries, with the exception of the one remark made by the Prince's uncle and first councillor, to the effect that the Shans had never ceded any territory whatever to any nation, and that they claimed the ancient boundaries of their State. What these ancient boundaries were he was unwilling, or possibly unable, to state.

The old boundary ran from a point on the Me Kong River, a little north of Maing Maing, in lat. 23° 30′, to Moung Ting, thence making a considerable bend north; it curved again south to Mine Mow and Nankan, and thence ran north-north-west, passing about 30 miles east of Bhamo and Talaw.

At present the boundary appears to be starting from a point on the Me Kong River, in lat. 22° 30′, and making a slight curve south it runs north to within 10 miles of Kiang Ma: thence runs south-west for 60 miles, then turns north-west to Nankan and Mine Mow, and thence runs nearly due north.

The people of Kiang Tung were most apathetic

and unconcerned about their borders, and what information I gained was from Yunnan traders. When I pointed out to the Prince's uncle that they were losing ground all round, that the Chinese were encroaching from the north and the Siamese from the south, he merely yawned, and said, "Are they?" as if the loss of territory was quite a minor detail. However, in further conversation he declared, as above stated, that no land, either north or south, had been ceded to any one, and that Kiang Tung still claimed sovereignty up to the limits of the old boundaries. It will therefore lie between Her Majesty's Government, the Emperor of China, and the King of Siam to settle these boundaries. From a British point of view, the sooner this settlement is made the better, for every year will see British territory beyond the Salween diminishing. Up to the present time encroachments have been made with impunity, and success begetting boldness, a few years of delay may make the work of a Boundary Commission both difficult and dangerous.

From the south the King of Siam, in the persons of the Laos of Chiengmai (Zimmé), has pushed his frontier quietly and peaceably to the Me Tsai River, 45 miles north of the old boundary.

The old boundary on this side, according to the

same authority, was formerly—starting from Dahthoteen on the Salween River and running fairly straight north-east for 70 miles to the junction of the Me Phang and Me Khok Rivers, thence making a sweep southwards, it follows the general direction of the Me Khok River, till it joins the Me Khong River, south of Kiangtsen.

The new boundary claimed by Siam, and in actual occupation by the Laos of the tributary State of Chiengmai (Zimmé), instead of following the line of the Me Khok River, makes a semi-circular sweep northwards, and taking the general line of the Me Tsai River, runs to the junction of the Me Phang and Me Khok Rivers. This encroachment not only includes the important town of Kiangtsen, but a well-watered and rich plain about 60 miles long and 45 miles broad.

The Kiang Tung people entirely repudiate this encroachment, but appear to have taken no steps to resist it. This is not so much from fear—for the Shans are, I should think, a more martial race than the Laos—but rather from sheer apathy.

The only definite and undisputed boundary is to the west, where the Salween River forms a clear dividing line between Kiang Tung and Burmah.

It is scarcely realized by most Englishmen that our newly acquired kingdom of Burmah does, through its subsidiary State of Kiang Tung, actually touch Tonquin, and through Tonquin the French. In other words, the English and French possessions in the Indo-Chinese peninsula are now contiguous.

At present, however, they are only contiguous on the map, and many hundred miles of unsettled and mountainous country separate the possessions of England and France.

The actual boundary line between Tonquin and Kiang Tung is a matter of conjecture. If we intend to maintain our inherited suzerainty over Kiang Tung, it would be both wise and politic, in conjunction with the French, to definitely settle her boundaries in this direction at as early a date as possible.

If, on the contrary, it is the intention of the British Government to sanction the continuance of the practical state of independence in which this province has existed during the last eight years—and I cannot help thinking that this would be the most far-sighted policy—it would be well to declare so at once.

The arguments in favour of this latter step are many and cogent.

E 2

The arguments in favour of the retention of this province are few and unimportant.

Our new kingdom of Burmah proper, bound as it is on the east by the Salween River flowing through high and almost impassable mountains, is on that face a compact and defensible kingdom, offering serious natural obstacles to invasion, and having a clear and definite boundary between our possessions and those of our neighbours on that hand.

Add the state of Kiang Tung, and an element of weakness is at once introduced to the safety of our Burmese possessions—to wit, a long, straggling, ill-defined tongue of country, which runs between two foreign nations and ends on the borders of a third; a province open to invasion to all three of them—to China from the north, to Siam from the south, and to the French from the east—and separated from us, the actual possessors, by lofty and impassable ranges of mountains, and approachable only to an English army by passing through Siam or China.

The Kiang Tung province in the hands of the British can never be anything but a source of weakness to the integrity of the Burmese kingdom. It will, like the Irishman's coat-tails, be dragging along the ground, a constant challenge to outsiders to tread upon it.

The soundest policy would appear to be to hand over the province to the Chinese, not as a possession but as a tributary State, making certain stipulations for trade and defence against aggression favourable to British interests.

The government of the province of Kiang Tung is carried on by a hereditary Prince, assisted by four councillors or magistrates.

The present Prince is only a child of twelve years old, who succeeded his father at the beginning of the year (1887). When I was in Kiang Tung in March, he had not yet been crowned, that ceremony being postponed till after the cremation of his father, which does not take place till six months after his death.

Of course the child is a mere puppet in the hands of the four councillors, though they prostrate themselves before him in public, and never approach him except in that grovelling position peculiar to Indo-Chinese nations.

He is a thin, pale, and rather idiotic-looking youth, with a face that may turn into a very cruel one. His father was an implacable enemy to all foreigners, and would not allow them to enter his domains. The American missionaries had made several attempts to obtain permission to visit Kiang Tung, but without success. The chief councillor informed me confidentially that I should not have lived a day if I had been unlucky enough to arrive two months earlier, during the lifetime of the old Prince.

The whole legislative and magisterial government is carried on by the four councillors, all of whom must be blood relations of the Prince. The chief councillor, who is Lord Chief Justice, is the most influential man in the province; he is a brother of the old Prince and uncle of the present ruler. One of the four councillors would command the army in case of war, but would probably direct their movements from his own house in Kiang Tung.

The penalty for murder and theft is death by beheading. Adultery and such like peccadilloes are not considered serious legal offences, but the injured man is at perfect liberty to pursue and kill both of the offending parties. Jealousy does not seem to be a ruling feature of the Shan character, and a money compensation is generally sufficient to soothe the feelings of the outraged husband. A rich man can always buy himself off from any punishment, even after committing murder or theft, care being taken not to insult the Lord Chief Justice by offering him too small a bribe.

The great preponderance of women at once strikes a traveller on entering Kiang Tung. I believe they do, as a fact, number a good many more than the men, but one's ideas of the excess of females is perhaps exaggerated on account of the whole of the marketing being done by them, bringing them more *en évidence* than their men.

The Shan, like the Pathan, has a bad reputation for treachery, and the Chief Justice informed me, with becoming pride, that they had never allowed an Englishman to leave the country alive. This was untrue, because I believe Captain McLeod passed through this place fifty years ago. The Chief Justice stoutly denied this.

In physique the Shan is a slight, wiry man, seldom more than five feet eight inches high, a splendid walker, mountaineer, and forester. Even when carrying heavy loads, bhangy-wise, a party of Shans kept up with our mules, the whole way from Zimmé to Kiang Tung, at an average rate of over twenty miles a day, over all sorts of country. In face he is small and wizen as a rule, with no moustache to speak of, and no hair on other parts of his person. The Prince asked me how old I was; I said 27, whereupon they all laughed, and candidly informed me that I was lying. There is a strain of Chinese blood in their veins, perhaps more noticeable in the faces of the women than the men. The men seem surly and distant in their manners, and I made friends with no one except a young merchant who joined us on the road. He, on the contrary, was rather too affectionate, and was constantly embracing me, at the same time combining business with pleasure by carefully feeling all over me to find out where I kept my money. I was warned on this point beforehand, that if it got known I had money, our lives were not worth a moment's purchase; consequently I lived night and day for three weeks with nearly two hundred pounds in gold-leaf and silver on my person. We pretended to be very poor, carrying out the farce so far as to bring the man from whom we bought three ponies in Kiang Tung right down to the Siamese territory before we paid him, on the plea that all our money was at Kiang Hai, the border town. Moungkin, a Burman in Kiang Tung, gave the inhabitants a very bad name. He had been there two years, and said that the laws

A gentleman who followed me like a shadow at Kiang Tung

A Lady who didnt'

A Wah hill man

A Mongson Hill woman

to face p. 57.

were not rigorously enforced, and the loss of life was lightly regarded. As mentioned above, the whole Burmese Embassy were murdered in cold blood a few years previously.

The women are very fair, and many of them pretty; but, as in other Eastern countries, they age very quickly. They nearly all have the Tartar cast of features. Their morals are as good as those of the Western nations—perhaps better, if anything. In figure they are medium-sized and plump, but they do not expose their persons as much as the Laos do in the street. Their gait is not elegant, like that of Indian women, but a regular waddle, caused by carrying water and other heavy loads on a banghy pole. Their costume consists of a small white linen jacket and a lungi, or sarong, used as a petticoat, and reaching below the knees. Their hair is long, and drawn into a knot on top of the head, and kept in place by a puggri of silk or cotton. On top of this, when out of doors, they wear an enormous hat, neatly made of reeds and bamboos. Only the higher classes wear small sandals, which protect the toes and half of the foot; the majority of women go barefooted.

The men wear a linen jacket, generally white, and

very loose dark-blue trousers, reaching to near the ankles. Their hair, like the women's, is long and gathered in a knot over one ear, being tied there by a silk handkerchief. Out of doors they wear huge straw hats beautifully made, and affording excellent shade and protection from the sun. The whole turn-out is a very serviceable and comfortable dress, with the drawback that there are no pockets. Very few men wear sandals or shoes.

A ready-made wife can be bought for Rs. 50. This is an excellent investment, for his wife, if properly managed, will repay her husband double that amount in a year by the work of her hands. Indeed, the Lord Chief Justice's head concubine, an old lady, can in five days weave a silk lungi valued locally at Rs. 18. The marriage-ceremony appears to be very simple; after the preliminaries have been settled and the guests for the marriage-feast assembled, the bride throws a cake of rice at the bridegroom, whereupon they become one.

The Shans of Kiang Tung, unlike the Laos, bury their dead as a rule, and only cremate very exalted personages. Perhaps this may be accounted for by the comparative scarcity of fuel, for the religion of the Shans and Laos is the same, viz. Buddhist.

As regards the martial qualities of the Shans, those who were fighting against them in Upper Burmah will be more qualified to judge than I am. They appeared to me vastly superior to the Laos and Siamese in that respect, and being accustomed to bear arms from boyhood, should be more proficient in their use than the soft agricultural races who inhabit the well-watered valleys of Siam. The two races, *i.e.* the Shans and Siamese, of which Laos is a tributary province, bear much the same relation to each other that the Pathans from the border hills on our North-West frontier bear to the Hindus of the plains of Bengal. Here, as in other parts of the world, the mountaineer is superior to the man of the plains in martial qualities. As an instance, perhaps the following incident throws some light on the character of the Shan. I had dismounted at a small hamlet outside Kiang Tung to make a sketch of a hut, and, finding my pony troublesome, held out the reins to a Shan amongst a group of people standing by, and asked him to hold my pony a minute. Instead of immediately complying, as a Laos would have done, he drew his knife on me, and poured forth a volley of abuse, which I was not sufficiently a master of the language to understand. Being entirely alone,

I thought it wisest to laugh the matter off, and, producing my revolver quite quickly, jocularly pointed out to him that I was six to one too good for him, whereupon he put up his knife and joined in the general laugh at his own expense. We parted good friends.

As noted in the description of Zimmé, the origin of the fond idea that a Shan is bullet-proof is to be found in the campaign against the Laos, when by mutual consent no bullets were used by either side.

There is a Chief Commissioner of Police, with a force of 150 constables. These are not *en évidence* at all, and do not wear any uniform. They do no patrolling or regular duty, but are used more like our "special constables" for apprehending criminals. I do not think they are very active in the discharge of their duties. Whilst in Kiang Tung my basin, tooth-mug, and tooth-brush were stolen. The penalty for theft here, as in Laos, being death, I asked the Chief Commissioner if he would kill the man who stole my tooth-brush. He said, "Certainly, *if you will catch him!*"

On entering Kiang Tung I met a Moulmein Burman who has been here three years, and talks a

A fellow Traveller

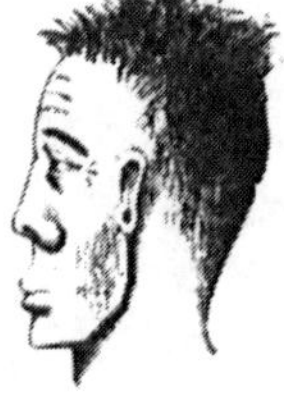

His twin brother

A Chinaman of Kiang Tung

A Kareen Child. aged 3 years

A Kareen

to face p. 60.

little Hindustanee. With him I called on the uncle of the Prince (the Prince being away), a nice, merry old gentleman, who was very much surprised to see me. Only once did things look unpleasant. He was making copious notes about me, my name, occupation, &c., when he suddenly asked, "Did I belong to the lot who were fighting the Shans between this and Mandalay?" The Burman answered, "Oh, dear, no, this is a gentleman who is travelling all over the world! He came in a ship to Moulmein, and when he gets to Bangkok he gets into another ship, and goes to some other country." The old gentleman, who did not look at all a nice old gentleman when he asked the question, became all smiles and good humour, and gave me a house to live in—a rather imposing-looking brick and plaster building, viewed from without. Within, it was like a rather inferior Indian stable. From what I gather, I don't think the rulers and people generally dislike the English, but many men from here have gone to Moné to fight against us as free lances, not sent by the Prince. I don't think they at all understand that whereas they were tributary to King Theebaw before, they are now tributary to us.

The Burman Moungkin came next day to say he

had been talking with the Prince's uncle, whom I visited yesterday. The uncle said, "The English are very bad people; what does this ruffian want here? No one travels in this country for pleasure" (as indeed they would not).

Moungkin in a blue funk came to me. I told him to say I was travelling around to enlarge my mind; that if my presence was considered an intrusion, I was quite willing to betake myself to a more hospitable country.

That afternoon Moungkin came to say the Prince would see me. First we went to the court house, a large wooden house on very high piles. At the end of the Hall of Justice was a large gilded thing that looked like a horse-trough with an over-mantle behind it. In front of this, a little lower, were two or three little stools which the Shans use for resting their elbows on while sitting on the ground. The gilded trough was therefore, I take it, merely a local emblem of justice. The judges sat in front of it. My friend the uncle was Lord Chief Justice, and there were three others. He asked my age, and would not believe I was a day under 40, which apparently is the age at which a Shan gets a moustache that many an old lady of ours would put to shame. Next he asked my business; I answered as before.

Had any "Magistrate" sent me? How long did it take to get from *London* (very small print) to KIANG TUNG (largest type)? He then came down and felt me all over, and, unearthing my revolver from my pocket, insisted it should be unloaded at once, and not be taken at all into the presence of the Prince. Having a good stout stick and another weapon handy, I did so, and, under pretence of going home with the revolver, hid it in my cummerbund. One can't be too careful when it is one man against a hundred. On my return the cashmire chogah was handed round, and much admired. Then we went across to the Prince's palace, a wretched shanty, in no way to be compared to the Zimmé chiefs'. After passing a broad outer verandah, we came to the audience chamber, about thirty feet square malled. We all squatted round the edge and waited for his Royal Highness to appear through a curtained door. The furniture and ornaments were a very mixed collection, some very valuable and others very trumpery things. Large vessels of solid gold and silver stood about amongst the rubbish of a Moulmein cheap-jack. A few spears and guns and an

English naval officer's sword on one side of the door, and a field officer's on the other. A gilt couch with room for two, and a curtain which could be dropped from the ceiling to hide it, stood in the corner by the door, and in front of it a mattress and some carpets, on which the Prince was to sit. He kept us waiting about fifteen minutes, during which time both my legs went to sleep. On his entrance they all prostrated themselves. The present Prince is only a child of twelve years old, who succeeded his father at the beginning of the year 1887. He is a thin-faced, long-nosed, foolish-looking youth.

My chogah was presented to him, and then they all began to jaw. I asked if they would like a railway; they said no, certainly not. In this conversation the youth took no part, but was busily engaged in trying to get a look at the chogah through a hole in the paper cover, as apparently it was not correct to do so before the donor. Nothing important was said or done, but after I arrived home a man came to say his Royal Highness wanted to see my gun and pistol. I took them up, but as his Royal Highness was much too exalted a personage to see the weapons in my hands, and as I stoutly refused to let them out of them, the young man had to do without, and

I went home. When I visited the Prince at Zimmé, he stood up, shook hands, and was most affable. Here, no one approaches within ten paces of the Prince, and only then in the grovelling attitude peculiar to these natives.

The following day I was sent for to show my gun and pistols to the Prince. He showed me a Winchester rifle for which he had paid 300 Rs., and two tawdry French revolvers, which I strongly advised him never to fire. He asked me to show him how to make caps and gunpowder. The soldiers are all armed with smooth-bore flintlock guns made in villages in the vicinity; gunpowder comes from Bangkok.

I came across a Hindu said to have been a servant of Margary's, who was killed at Mauwyne in 1875. He lived in great style at first, had lots of money, and married a Shan woman—all probably with Margary's money. He is now poor, and his wife keeps him by selling cigarettes; he said he wanted to come along with me. He was constantly hanging about, trying to pump my servants as to what money or valuables I had.

Of course Judh Bir is as staunch as any Guide that ever stepped; but the Madrassi was in such a funk that he would have sold the two of us to save his own skin. Judh Bir and I did sentry by turns and never left the others alone a minute.

He is a famous little fellow, always merry and on the spot. I could not have had a better man of any nation. He was good for five of these evil-looking scoundrels if it had come to arms.

His broad, good-natured smile and sturdy mien was just what was wanted to keep back the unsavoury crowd which surrounded my billet at intervals during the day. Any ill temper or overbearing manner of a Pathan would at once have kindled the spark which would have brought out a hundred knives and ended us.

Before leaving Kiang Tung I may note the different modes of transport in use.

The Shans do not use ponies and mules for pack work; they confine themselves entirely to bullocks.

The Yunnans use nothing but ponies and mules. Their pack-saddle being unique I give a note on it.

The saddle is made of wood, the back of the animal being protected from it by three flaps, made of double canvas, and stuffed with raw rice so as to fit the animal. In case of an animal getting rubbed on the spine, a pad of numbdah is nailed along the bottom edge of the saddle, the effect being to raise it above the spine. In case of rub on either side of the animal, the rice is taken out of the flap, so as to leave a hollow opposite the wound, and the rice is kept from dropping back to its old place by stitching round the hollow.

No girths are used, and the saddle is kept in place by a broad gut breast-band and breaching strap.

Loads have in consequence to be adjusted absolutely exactly, or the whole thing, saddle and load, will fall off.

Loads are not placed directly on the saddle, but are made up on a trestle on the ground, and just before starting the whole load, trestle and all, is lifted on to the saddle. The trestle is made to fit into the groves of the saddle exactly, and balances itself there, but is not secured in any way. This trestle contrivance appeared to me excellent. In our service some of the first loaded transport animals are standing loaded for hours before they commence their day's labour, whereas here all the loads stand on their trestles on the ground, and at the order to march, three men load up the whole caravan of fifty ponies in two minutes and the animals start fresh and jolly.

The great advantage of the saddle—an advantage shared by the old "Punjab" pack-saddle used by the Guides—is the possibility of not only working animals with sore backs, but actually curing them whilst in work. My three pack ponies had fearful sore backs, but whilst marching 300 miles we cured them completely, our only medicine being pigs' fat.

The Yunnans give the ponies about 4 lb. of paddy per diem, divided into two feeds, one before starting for the morning march, and the second after the evening march. They water them twice during the day, once after the completion of the morning march about 11 A.M., and again before starting for the afternoon march at 1 o'clock.

During the whole night, and during the midday halt of three hours, all the ponies are turned out loose to graze without any guard or cordon to prevent their straying. When they are wanted, a gun is fired, a gong is beaten, and all the owners set up shrill calls, and the ponies come trotting in. Occasionally some ponies stray out of hearing, and have to be tracked out—at first a seemingly impossible task in the dense forest, but we very soon got very sharp at it. For the morning march the Yunnans start at daybreak and cover from nine to twelve miles, according to distances between grazing grounds. They then turn the ponies out to graze for three hours or so, and then cover another twelve miles before evening—this over the most difficult country. In fact, they make longer marches in the hills than in the plains, the reason for which I could not get out of them.

Immediately on arriving at a camping ground the loaded trestles are lifted to the ground, and by undoing one buckle the whole saddle and gear is stripped off the animal and he trots off to graze. Coming round a sharp corner, I have found the third pony in front of me unloaded, stripped, and grazing at the new camping ground.

The ponies are never groomed at all, and at night have no covering whatever. According to our views this stripping off of saddlery before the animal is cool is wrong. But the Yunnans having no commissariat to fall back on, find that they cannot afford to waste half an hour out of grazing time, whilst the animal is cooling down. I noticed no bad results from this system. As far north as Kiang Tung few bullock caravans are met, the whole trade being carried on with mules and ponies.

Bullock caravans mostly work from Zimmé *viâ* Kiang Hai to Kiangtsen on the Me Kong, and thence up the banks of that river to Kiang Hung. The Louai Chang Mountain, with its almost precipitous ascent, forms a barrier which prevents bullock traffic, on any extensive scale, reaching Kiang Tung from the south. On the march the bullocks move in single file, headed by a leader, gaily caparisoned, and covered with bells. The bullock bells are new to me; instead of having the striker inside the bell, they have one on each side *outside.* The bell is often a bit of hollow bamboo.

The merchants distribute themselves along the line, and drive their animals. The pace is very slow, scarcely two miles an hour under the most favourable circumstances; the day's march being from ten to twelve miles.

A bullock caravan starts at dawn, and makes its day's march straight on, generally reaching camp at about 11 A.M.; the bullocks are then turned out to graze for the rest of the day. At night they are collected and picquetted near their loads.

The pack saddle consists of two small sacks stuffed with straw, on which are securely lashed a pair of panniers 3½ ft. deep, and 1½ ft. in diameter, in which the merchandise is placed. The pack is placed well forward on the hump, and kept in its place by a breast-band in front and a breaching strap behind. No girths are used.

A Yunnan Mule
Driver

The original was rather
a pleasing looking little
damsel but again the
Printer and I have failed
to do her justice.

A leading pack bullock
f a caravan with a large
winging gong on the top
f the load.

to face p. 70.

An apparition met on the
road. The bandage round
the head is used by some
as protection from the sun.

The bullocks were generally in very good condition, and sore backs are rarely seen.

The elephant is used as a pack animal both in Siam and the Shan States, but owing to the peculiar construction of the howdah, only a very small load, in actual bulk, can be carried. This howdah is like a wooden cradle balanced crossways on the elephant's spine. It is 6 ft. long, 2 ft. broad and 2 ft. deep. Into this small space the whole load has to be packed. A traveller using this form of transport would do well, therefore, to have his luggage made up in small bundles; for not only does the size of the howdah make it difficult to stow away anything large, but the elephants, as a rule, being only half trained, will not sit down to be loaded, and consequently everything has to be handed up to the mahout, and packed into the howdah by him. The elephant is, I think, quite out of his element in the hills. He is born and bred in the plains, and there does excellent work In the hills his great intelligence carries him through difficulties, which it is hardly fair to put to a beast of his huge ungainly bulk, and he works under protest in a very slow and laboured way. His load, to enable him to do this work, is made so light as to be nothing more than a respectable mule-load.

The pad used with the elephant howdah is most primitive. It consists of four or five sheets, or rather planks made of flattened bamboos, each one yard square, and piled one on top of another. Before starting on a march the mahout wets the animal's spine with water.

The policy of the State of Kiang Tung with relation to neighbouring States appears to be one of complete isolation.

The Chinese are hated and feared, and their small settlement outside the town is merely tolerated as a necessary evil, which the Shans are afraid to get rid of by violence. In the same way the Yunnan traders are allowed to pass through on sufferance, and not from any friendly feeling. I asked the chief of my Yunnan caravan to come with me when I went to interview the Prince. He would not on any account, expressively drawing his finger across his throat to account for his unwillingness. Towards other foreigners the policy of the Kiang Tung Shans is equally hostile—impassively hostile, I think, but still hostile. By which I mean that they would never give their consent to a foreigner entering their country, but once he is there, they let him live on sufferance, reserving the right of butchering him in cold blood at a moment's notice if they feel so inclined.

The Shans of Kiang Tung, as mentioned above, are afraid of the Chinese, and being afraid to resent their encroachments, feign ignorance of them.

With the Laos the Shans of Kiang Tung are on anything but friendly terms, and the feeling is reciprocated. The Zimmé Prince would not give me a letter of introduction to the Prince of Kiang Tung, or in any way countenance my crossing the border, as he said that the latter was not his friend. No doubt he was afraid that if mischief befell us whilst bearing a friendly letter from him, that not only would his own prestige suffer in the eyes of both nations, but that he might get into trouble with the British authorities for aiding and abetting my entering a dangerous and hostile country. Anyhow it was quite apparent, both at Kiang Tung and at Zimmé, that there was no love lost between the two States, and the friendship which existed at the time of the friendly campaign has died out.

With regard to European nations and European politics, the Princes and people are hopelessly ignorant. According to their ideas there is only one white nation, called "Angrit" (English), which is split up into various tribes and States, such as the Americans, Londoners, dwellers in Calcutta, and so on.

Of the French they had never heard, and thought Lieutenant Garnier's French scientific expedition of 1868 was a party of Englishmen from Bangkok. It appears that six of Garnier's party came across from Muang Yu on the Me Kong River to the vicinity of Kiang Tung, and then rejoined the main body of the expedition at Kiang Hung. The Prince's uncle declared that they had been killed between Kiang Tung and Kiang Hung, and that all their clothes and goods had been exposed for sale in the market of the latter place. This of course was a lie.

They profess to have no fear of the British, pointing to the lofty ranges of mountains which divide Kiang Tung from the Salween as their defence.

A few years ago Kiang Hung was a separate principality, but was conquered by Kiang Tung and made subsidiary. Its population largely consists of Chinese, and its proclivities are certainly Chinawards.'

This may be from natural inclinations, but more probably on account of its situation on the frontier of that powerful nation, and to all intents and purposes under its thumb.

The only people that the State of Kiang Tung seems friendly with is the Shan State of Moné, to whose assistance they sent 3000 men to fight against the British.

I was surprised to find how little merchandise of any description came from China. The caravans working down towards Moulmein consisted of mules and ponies, four-fifths of which carried no loads whatever. Indigo, tea, and shoes appear to be the only things which come from China, and the demand for these is very small. What little the Yunnan traders bring down they dispose of at Kiang Tung, or at furthest at Zimmé, and continue the journey to Moulmein with unloaded mules. On the return journey from Moulmein they bring up every description of cheap cotton goods, bright coloured flannels, and odds and ends of trumpery. The people of Kiang Tung cannot afford to buy the more expensive cloths, as I found to my cost when, in my character of merchant, I tried to sell some that was worth at least Rs. 5 a yard in Calcutta. It would only fetch the price of the commonest flannels in Kiang Tung.

The only really lucrative trade which the Shans drive is the trade in ponies, erroneously called

Burmah ponies. These hardy little beasts, which are seldom more than 12-2 hands high, are bred chiefly in the Kiang Tung Valley. During the winter of 1886-87, about 500 ponies were sent to Rangoon and Moulmein. I was surprised to find prices so high, more especially as I arrived after all the pony caravans had started for Burmah, and what were left behind were presumably only animals unfit for the Moulmein market. Three-year-olds, standing from 11 hands to 12 hands high, were valued at from Rs. 40 to Rs. 80, all the colts being gelt or mulled. Three ponies, fit to carry a load, cost me Rs. 340, with their pack saddles thrown into the bargain; and I was offered Rs. 200 by a breeder for my own Shan pony, which cost Rs. 270 in Moulmein. Prices in Moulmein run from Rs. 120 to Rs. 250 for raw ponies straight from the Shan country. The ponies are led down the whole way barebacked, and without any covering at night. They arrive in excellent condition as a rule, and carry a very fine, good coat. During the marches through the hills they are fed almost entirely on bamboo leaves, getting a feed of paddy or a lump of goor whenever opportunity occurs.

The Burmah or Shan pony makes an admirable pack or draught animal; his splendid legs, indomitable pluck, and great powers of endurance compensate for his small size. As a hack, he can only be considered in the light of a means of conveyance, for riding paces he has none. He is generally bull-necked, and, consequently, has not a mouth worth mentioning, and his small size makes his trot and canter so short that they cause the rider unspeakable anguish. On the other hand, he is, as a rule, a very good walker. My opinion on his paces is given after an eighteen hundred miles' ride on all descriptions of Shan ponies. The breeding operations are not carried on under any system, one or two stallions being turned loose with a herd of mares. The introduction of small Arab or Indian stallions, not over 13-2 hands, would, in time, produce a very valuable breed of ponies. The Shan pony has already magnificent legs, and the girth of a 15-hand Indian horse. (The saddle and girths which I use for my first charger, an Arab standing 15-1 hands high, fitted my Shan pony exactly.) He wants the neck, mouth, and paces of other breeds.

Mules are not bred much in Kiang Tung; nearly all that are seen there come from Yunnan. They cost about 20 per cent. more than ponies, and anything over 13 hands costs Rs. 200 and upwards. Their general size is 12 hands to 12-2 hands, of a good stamp, and for their size quite equal to mules in other parts of the world. The Punjab mule is, however, finer, stronger, and cheaper.

There is no local coinage, the British rupee being the standard coin of the province. As in Laos, we noticed here that the smaller coins, such as 2-anna and 4-anna bits, bear a higher relative value than the rupee; that is, one can buy as much, if not more, for seven 2-anna bits than for a rupee. No copper coins of any description are current; but amongst themselves the market women use strings of split betel-nuts in lieu of them, or else barter their goods one with another, according to the present market value of their small stock. The British 8-anna piece is not current, and will only be taken at the value of a 4-anna piece. No gold coins are current, but gold leaf is used instead. It is, however, more looked on as a form of merchandise than a fixed value coin. For instance, a tical of gold costing in Zimmé Rs. 30, in Kiang Tung would not fetch more than Rs. 28. The current value may be Rs. 28-8, but the purchaser requires to make his own small profit on the transaction. For a traveller this is the only portable form in which money can be carried.

British currency notes it may be possible to change through the courtesy of some of the Europeans at Zimmé, but north of that they are not current at all. With regard to silver it is advisable to carry as much as possible in 2-anna and 4-anna pieces. In the small villages, where change is scarce, one often would have to pay a rupee for an article which was only valued at 2 annas, and which the villager would gladly sell at that price, but he has no change, or does not care to part with it.

Owing to the scarcity and dearness of powder, the Shans are not a sporting race.

On the lakes and ponds, both inside and outside of the walls of Kiang Tung, duck, teal and moor-hens may be seen entirely at their ease, and not in the least afraid of human beings. Snipe are very plentiful in all the marshy patches which surround the town on all sides.

About four miles north-east of Kiang Tung is a small lake or large pond, on which are many water-fowl of all sorts.

I saw no signs of large game of any sort, but was told that there are a few deer in the hills. We came across two leopards, but did not get a shot at either.

In the hills between Me Tsau and Hai Tuk, we met a party of Kareen hunters with cross-bows and poisoned arrows: they had had no sport that day. We heard that they could kill elephants and hippopotami with their poisoned arrows.

CHAPTER V.

RETURN JOURNEY TO UTARADIT.

Leave Kiang Tung on return journey—At Kiang Hai again—A growl—No police required—No made roads—Sunday halt at Muang Nan—Purchase sapphires—The results thereof—Sapphire story—Muang Nan on the Me Nan River—Ponies troublesome—Siamese diet uninviting—Two Shan boys—Prince's visit at Muang Nan—Rocket entertainment—Poungi's house under repair—Leave Muang Nan—Reach Utaradit—Siamese letter—Lodge at the post-office—Natives' ideas of distance hazy—Sunday rest—Education in Siam—Costume in Siam and Laos—Many wives doubtful blessing—Personal appearance after three months' march.

On the 19th of March we left Kiang Tung with a party of Yunnans and retraced our steps, recrossing the Nouai Chang (Elephant Mountain) next day. All the mules except mine were unloaded, consequently ran down the whole way, and did the twelve miles in three hours. Some devilment was up here, and Judh Bir and I sat very tight, relieving one another at night. At the midday halt our headman, after talking some time with a Shan whom we met, came to me and said he and his caravan were going back to Kiang Tung, as he heard it was raining at Zimmé. This was rather a facer for us. Luckily I owed him Rs. 200, part payment of the ponies which I had promised to pay him at Kiang Hai (as it was our policy to appear very poor at Kiang Tung). Ananias, my boy—who certainly is the most fearful, hopeless coward God ever created—was thrown into such a blue perspiring funk at the bare idea of our going on alone, that he went off and used all his wiles, and no doubt thousands of lies, with the headman, and finally induced him to come on. During the afternoon we passed several caravans, all toiling along as hard as they could, and at night I noticed, instead of allowing the ponies out to graze, they were stacked close, and pickets posted about 200 yards up the road.

Some prowling band of Shans probably had been seen or heard of about: hence our friend's excuse about the rain at Zimmé.

We were a tight little party, and the Chinamen are first-rate fellows. It might have fared badly with us alone, with that skunk Ananias as a thorn in our side. The Zimmé Shan servant, too, does not look up to much warfare.

On the 25th of March we got back to Kiang Haî, having had three days' regular downpour. Both times we passed Kiang Haî there were heavy thunderstorms, the rain lasting this time three days; thermometer varying from about 66–62° at night to 81–85° in the daytime.

Eyes inflamed from heat and glare, together with a bad festering sore on the leg, caused by the bite of a dog, seems at this time to have disturbed my naturally serene temperament, as will appear from the following extract from my journal:—

"This is what I call real enjoyment; some people might hate it, but we just revel in it, don't we, my faithful squire, Judh Bir? We split a chicken for dinner, and carefully put by a leg for to-morrow's midday meal. With lots of rice, and washed down with dirty water, it is a diet fit for the gods! We sleep where and how we can, under a tree, a bamboo stack, or an old hut. About an hour before dawn Judh Bir fires a gun, not to announce another joyous day, but to frighten away any leopards prowling about and also as a signal for the ponies to come in from grazing. This gun always drives me to utter unparliamentary language. The ponies are very good and generally come in quickly, but sometimes when grass is scanty they stray out of gunshot hearing, and then we have a pleasant little trudge of three or four miles tracking them. The ponies loaded, off we start. A Shan and the Madrassi first, then the ponies, then Judh Bir and the other Shan, and last I and my pony. They go along very well, over three miles an hour when they have had decent grazing and grain.

"I have to dismount every twenty minutes and hang my leg up in a tree; riding makes all the blood run down into it, and it becomes quite a decent leg for a young elephant.

"I take this opportunity to take my bearings and make notes. My eyes are much better; for a long time I had to use them by turns, giving one a rest under a bandage—the result of sun and dirt, I suppose!

"The middle of the day we put up under a tree for three or four hours, and turn the ponies to graze. Nothing so delightful, my dear sir, as to take a book and your pipe and lie under a shady tree and revel in the luxury of idleness—as long as you don't have too much of it. Believe me an armchair in the club smoking-room is preferable. Under your tree the sun is constantly changing, and before you have been five minutes in one spot, specially chosen with much forethought as bound to remain shady all day, the sun is full on you. The only book you have you have read a dozen times, and know by heart. Your tobacco is dry and burns your tongue, and every species of venomous winged insect comes with one accord and worries you. About two o'clock we move on again and do as much as we can before dark. Then I generally get fever and go to bed. Judh Bir cooks his dinner and follows me. And so the happy days spin round. The ponies, poor devils, have a wretched time with large stinging flies, which give them not a moment's peace, and won't allow them to graze."

A very peaceful, well-ordered people these must be, for there is not a sign of a soldier or policeman in the land.

The courts of justices in the few places where there are any, appear to be always empty—not, I hope, because Justice is absent, but because there is no one that wants that estimable female.

Throughout Siam, as far as we have seen 1000 miles or so, there are no made roads at all. The most important towns are connected only by mere footpaths, worn by pack animals and passengers. These paths are never straight for fifty yards together, and in forest land wind very much. This of course makes the distances between places much greater than need be.

You never see two men walking side by side, but always one behind the other, though they may be traversing a plain five miles wide, where they might walk 500 abreast. Beyond felling a tree across it, or pulling a couple of bamboos for foot passengers, no attempt is made at bridging the numerous streams and swamps.

Occasionally in the middle of a village a rude bridge is thrown across, but is seldom safe for pack animals.

About two marches before we reached Muang Nan we were halting for our Sunday rest at a small wayside village. We were particularly happy that day, having had a square meal of stewed fowl, eggs, and plantains, after a week of severe marching on little or no food, and were sitting in the village school smoking pipes and enjoying the view and the complete rest and laziness of the position, when a small boy came up with a mysterious little packet of rags, out of which he proceeded to produce a collection of polished stones and pebbles of all sorts. We took a languid interest in the first few produced,

A Shan Merchant of Kiang Tung who joined us on the road.

A Poungi or priest

A fascinating youth at Muang Nan one of the jeunesse doré the dissipated son of the Commissioner.

to face p: 86.

—they were common crystals, though beautifully polished; but later, when he began to ladle out sapphires of the finest water and valued them at the same price as his crystals, dreams of boundless wealth swam before our eyes. We bought up every sapphire the village contained, eighteen in all, at an average price of about one shilling apiece. None of us were experts in stones, but it required only the most uneducated eye to see that these stones were of great value. The natives showed us exactly where they got them from, and we made a careful map of the place, and worked out its exact longitude and latitude. I suppose all of us have built castles in the air on the foundations of suddenly and unexpectedly acquired wealth: we have settled exactly what we would do with our money. A nice little place in the country, a hunting box in one of the best hunting centres, a yacht, shooting trips to all parts of the world, and so on. And here were we the actual possessors of a secret which meant boundless wealth; the sole discoverers of a spot where sapphires were as cheap as marbles; a spot out of the track of traders, and never before visited by a white man. It was surprising how quietly we took our good fortune: we might still have been the ordinary penniless subaltern and his soldier orderly instead of two men with princely fortunes within their grasp. Our only regret was that we should have to leave the old regiment: it is impossible to soldier and also manage a large fortune, and so, reluctantly enough, we decided that we must go. I cannot imagine how a man with a large fortune can stand the petty annoyances which it appears to be the aim and object of military organizers to inflict on the British officer. The civilian reader perhaps hardly realizes the pettiness and unsuitableness of some of the work exacted from an officer. That very fine fellow you have just seen walking down the street, with a gold hat balanced on the top of his ear, a scion of nobility, a public school man and a graduate at Oxford, has just been inspecting a large supply of raw meat and recording his valuable opinion as to its suitability or otherwise for human food. He is now on his way to poke about the cookhouses, and later on will go round and ask every man in the regiment if he has any complaints to make about his food. The idea is that an officer is a very lazy fellow, and, having no duties of his own to perform, it is necessary to request him to perform the combined duties of a butcher, a sanitary subordinate, and a lance-corporal, just to keep him in fettle and in fit condition to lead Her Majesty's soldiers against the foreign foe.

But I have drifted rather away from our sapphire mine and our fortune. For three months we were the richest men in the world, and on reaching Calcutta I at once took the samples we had to the leading jeweller and asked his opinion of them. After a long and careful examination of each in detail, he murmured gently as he gazed at the last of the lot through a spy-glass: "Lovely colour, light perfect, not a flaw, would be worth 50 guineas apiece, if" —shutting up his spy-glass—"they were not made of Birmingham paste."

I left that shop full of burning indignation against Birmingham and all its ways. I don't so much mind the untutored savage being stuck with Birmingham sapphires, but I do most strongly object to having the joke passed on to me in an unknown and unexplored country thousands of miles away from Birmingham and the white man's civilization.

I was asking the same jeweller in Calcutta if any officers had brought back good rubies from Burmah.

"Yes, sir, lots of very fine ones, but, bless you, they are all made of paste."

"What! Birmingham again?"

"Yes, sir, Birmingham again!"

We came across another sapphire story. I think it was Mr. Gould told it us. At Chantabong, a couple of hundred miles east of Bangkok, there are some well-known sapphire mines, which are regularly worked and give a very fair yield. Strolling down towards these mines one day, the narrator met one or two miners returning from their day's labour. He stopped and asked them what luck they had had. "Oh! so so," producing two or three chunks of exceedingly uninteresting-looking stone.

"What will you take for one of those?" "Forty dollars." Seeing the buyer rather taken aback at the largeness of the price asked for an unpolished and uncut stone, the miner put it back in his pocket and began to move off in a nonchalant manner. My friend, seized with a sudden mania for possessing the stone, planked down his dollars and took it home to an expert. It proved to be of glass, manufactured in Birmingham, sent out to the sapphire mines and buried there! for when my friend bought it, it was covered with mud, and had evidently just come out of the ground.

On the 12th of April we reached Muang Nan, a walled town on the Me Nan River.

There had been heavy rains, which made it cooler, otherwise it is hot and muggy. April is considered the hottest month in these parts. We seem to have pursued the "hottest month" with much vigilance. At Kiang Tung we caught him, and now again. At Muang Nan there is no regular bazaar, only a daily market attended almost solely by women. Outside the north-east corner of the town are sheds, in which caravan men sell cheap cotton and silk goods. The whole trade at this season is done by bullocks, the river not being navigable above Muang Pak, about five miles south of this place. This is considered a very cheap country for buying elephants; I met several Burmans from Moulmein looking out for them. The only other means of transport are bullocks, and of these we met many hundreds on the road between this and Kiang Hai.

The Me Nan is a much larger river than the Me Ping at Zimmé. The Me Nan comes in from a generally northern direction. It is a fine stream, with broad beds and high banks, capable of holding

5 or 6 ft. more water at the ford. At this season it was not navigable even for river boats; only half a dozen small dingies were to be seen.

There are no timber forests anywhere near, but many logs were lying about, showing that there is timber not far off.

After parting company with the Yunnans, for some weeks we had endless trouble with the ponies, constantly losing them at night, and even sometimes during the midday halt. It was generally the fault of the imp Joe, my pony. He used to swagger around and give himself airs before the other ponies, because he did not carry a load, and they, like their human fellow-creatures, taking him at his own valuation, bowed down to him and followed him about everywhere like sheep. Joe, not being accustomed to liberty, used to walk off in a jaunty way into the forest and lose his way, and the other three, who if alone could find their way back to camp through any country, blindly followed him. When he pulled up hopelessly lost, they pulled up too, and waited beside him till we tracked them out. After a short time we got quite sharp at this tracking work, and often tracked out ponies four or five miles through dense forest and jungle; we could tell our own ponies' tracks from others and could distinguish each pony's track from those of its fellows. Judh Bir was much better at it than I was, and his cleverness in recognising which pony was leading often enabled us to make long casts ahead and shortened our labours considerably. If Joe was leading, we might have to go anywhere and any distance; if the small bay mare was leading, she generally went for the best grazing she had passed during the last march, and so on with each one of the four. One day I remember, during a midday halt, the bay mare took them back very nearly to the last camp, where there had been particularly succulent grazing. It must not be supposed that we always had this work before marching: the rule was to find the ponies waiting for their grain close round our bivouac when we woke, and the exception to have to track them out. Ananias used to start off with the greatest energy when any tracking was to be done, and choosing a snug corner in the forest a few hundred yards off would lie down there until he heard the pistol shot announcing that the ponies had reached camp. Judh Bir caught him at that game once, and would have skinned him alive if I had not interfered. The ponies are turned out to graze without halters or anything on them, and are as safe from theft as most things can be. We often tried to catch them at off-times when out grazing, by way of experimentalizing in horse-stealing, but always failed ignominiously. Feeding time is the only time to catch them, and woe betide the wretched traveller if one is let slip again after he has finished his grain; the best part of the day may be spent in trying to catch him again. Whenever this did happen we used to lie down resignedly and wait till the little beast chose to come up and be caught, for it only made one hot and profane dodging about after him, whilst he was enjoying the fun immensely. If we refused to play, he generally shut up pretty quick, for it takes two people to appreciate a joke.

One of the chief Siamese articles of diet is dried fish. They cut them open and hang them up in the sun till they smell worse than a crowd of dead camels, then they eat them. A most astonishing race from a dietary point of view; they live on a collection of the most unwholesome things that the mind of man can imagine. In addition to the above-mentioned luxury, they feed on red chillies, taken whole and by the dozen; any other herbs that are sufficiently fiery or pungent, garlic and rice. Between meals they alternately chew betel, which is about as hot as anything out of Hades, and smoke hot strong tobacco made up into cigarettes about the size and shape of a posthorn.

If his Satanic Majesty has any warmer diet to put them on in the realms below, I am sure they will take kindly to it.

We engaged two Shan boys as servants during part of the journey, one to look after the ponies and one to forage for supplies. They were both very ignorant of their work, but both very willing at starting, and under Judh Bir's firm but comfortable rule one of them turned out an excellent servant. Judh Bir corrupted their names into "Sam" and "Combien," which however answered quite as well as their real ones, which were long and unpronounceable. Sam was the one who turned out a trump, contrary to expectation, for Combien was much the smartest lad at starting. It turned out, however, that he was a confirmed opium smoker, and when he had run out of the small supply he had with him he fell to pieces. With opium he was a smart active servant; without it a wretched old dyspeptic, fit for nothing. Another infirmity of his was a natural greediness, which led him to eat anything and everything he could lay hands on. Every hut we passed he got something eatable out of, probably saying it was for me. All these little delicacies he used to put into little bamboo buckets and sling them about his person, so that at the end of a march he was a perfect Christmas tree of bamboo buckets. On arrival in camp he used to set to work and eat all these dainties one after another, generally finishing up quite strong on the remains of my gruesome meal. He was then comfortably sick and went to sleep. After a fortnight I sacked him, for his bestial ways were quite unbearable.

These Shan boys had no caste prejudices, and would eat or drink anything, and put their hands to any kind of work. Sam used to help make up the loads each morning, and then tracking out the ponies would drive them in and give them their morning feed, saddling them meanwhile. All day he led our little caravan and was responsible for leading us right, no easy matter through thick forest with paths running in all directions. On arrival in camp he used to help unload and unsaddle the ponies, and then went off foraging for food and grain, often returning empty-handed after a couple of hours' search.

He required no transport for his personal kit,

carrying his little all on his person. Ananias, on the contrary, required rather more than I did myself; I actually found one bulky carpet bag of his which contained a feather pillow, which we had carried for about 1000 miles for him. I nearly committed murder on the person of Ananias with that pillow when I discovered it. Each of the Shan boys, in addition to his own kit, carried a carbine, whilst Ananias, for reasons before set forth, preferred to carry the poles of my cot. They were all wonderful walkers, never seemingly coming to the end of their powers; but they were very weak in the arms, and made a great to do of lifting a load on to a pony.

At Muang Nan the Prince's son came to see me, a pleasant, civil youth with one eye, who seemed delighted to meet me. I thought at first he mistook me for some one else, till it transpired that he had been to Bangkok and there imbibed a lasting admiration for Englishmen and all things English. This admiration extended even to the homely "solah topee" of my nation, his costume consisting of a linen patrol jacket, a silk loin-cloth, lavender-coloured stockings, boots, and a very dirty pith hat; the whole turn-out making up a sort of cross between a poor Eurasian and a Bengali Babu in boots. I should certainly have taken him for something of that sort, if I had not noticed the people grovelling before him as he came along. We talked about roads and ways and means, and got on very well together.

The people of Nan look like and dress like the Zimméites, in fact they are merely a political division of the same race. The women wear their hair knotted rather higher up on their heads. The men are much addicted to drink, judging from the number of jolly fellows we saw being conveyed to the bosoms of their families at all hours of the night and day: "kinloh" they call it. There is the same lavish display of the female form divine here as elsewhere in the Laos States, but I don't know that their morals are any the worse for that.

The greater part of the male population, including a large sprinkling of priests, seem to spend their days in letting off huge rockets. The largest was a 30-ft. bamboo as thick as my arm. This bit of timber was launched into the air by the agency of a whole cluster of bamboo powder-flasks lashed to its head. These firework parties start off in the morning for some open space, taking several rockets of all sizes, a band of music, and plenty of "kinloh." There they proceed to let off the rockets and drink the "kinloh," to the accompaniment of the dulcet strains of their band. Towards evening they return to the town very noisy and happy. This noise and happiness they keep up the greater part of the night. The women are quiet and industrious, and do not participate at all in these jovial gatherings. Poungies (priests) here, as everywhere in Siam, abound, wearing the same yellow clothes as in Burmah. They have the character of being a dissolute lot, but we met with nothing but kindness from them.

Whilst we were at Muang Nan they were building or repairing a big poungi (priest's) house. In this work all the people assisted, men, women, and children. The lower classes worked all day, on and off, and in the cool of the evening the "upper ten" turned out to do their share, each and all according to their rank, in a gradually diminishing degree. Fine ladies of exalted rank brought back a handful of sand after taking their evening bath in the river; a portly old gentleman, in a red headpiece, evidently a Royal Duke at least, a pocket-handkerchief full of the same; the Prince's nephew (a blear-eyed youth, who called in on us on a chance of getting a drink) carried up a large bagful; and so on, each according to his rank aiding in the pious labour.

In every village is a poungi house, with a separate house for travellers, where we usually put up. They generally have an altar with a lot of small gilt "Buddhas" on them, each with a little shawl on, and a chunk of rice in front of it. There seems to be no fanaticism about the people. We infidels eat and sleep before the altar of their gods with their full consent.

The village school is generally held in this guest-house, as it is seldom occupied in the daytime.

On the 16th of April we started from Muang Nan, following the right bank of the Me Nan River as far as Muang Sa—the road was the same as we came by. The river, though broad and deep, is fordable in many places, the water being 2 ft. to 3 ft. deep, the current slow, and the bottom sand and mud.

In many places a wicker fence is made across the river, with two or three fishing platforms along it on raised piles. From the height of these platforms it is evident that the river does not rise more than 3 or 4 ft. in the rains. From these platforms they fish with square hand-nets about 4 ft. square.

We reached Muang Phang on the 24th of April; next day brought us to Utaradit, on the Me Nan River. The road for the last thirty miles had been very difficult, in many parts never having been used before for anything but passenger traffic and elephants. The path through the dense bush was so narrow that the ponies could scarcely push their way through it, and the ascent and descent out of the river and water-courses were often so steep and narrow that the ponies had to be unloaded, and their loads carried up and down.

Utaradit is a long straggling place, extending for more than a mile along the right bank of the river, the houses being dotted in a dense bush forest. Along the river are moored many hundred boats, in which a great portion of the population appear to live. These boats are large, with the dwelling part closed on every side. I saw one or two huts on rafts and piles. It was very difficult here to procure eatables, there being apparently no daily market.

Tobacco is cultivated here on an extensive scale along the low-lying bits of the river-bank, but little or no paddy is grown, owing to the difficulty in clearing the jungle.

At Utaradit the Siamese Commissioner's son frequented me a good deal. He was a very dissipated, boiled gooseberry-eyed-looking youth, with a majestic air: but he was kind enough to say that he did not think me a bad chap. I am ashamed to say that I had not the presence of mind to return the compliment. He afforded me a great deal of amusement one way and another, for which I was grateful. The facial gymnastics he put himself through when speaking were alone a play, and quite sufficient to have made his fortune as a low comedian across the river at home. He was, I was led to suppose, one of the *crème de la crème* of Bangkokian society. No doubt the semi-extinct English "masher" would have seemed quite as funny to him as he did to me.

A Siamese letter is about two yards long by one foot broad, and folds up like a fire-screen. The paper is black and the pencil white. When folded up for transmission, it is securely corded up with a bit of rope; and a fid of clay about two inches in diameter is affixed to the knot by way of a seal. An English "Mail" from London to Bombay, if it was composed of letters on the Siamese pattern, would sink the largest P. and O. afloat.

On arrival at Utaradit we turned into the first empty shed available; this proved to be the Post Office, a rickety shanty with a large red letter-box lashed to a massive centre post by a wisp of bamboo. We were wondering why some one did not take the opportunity, when the box was full of money orders, to walk off boldy with his Majesty's mails, pillar-box and all. On examination, however, it proved that the lid of the aperture through which the weighty correspondence of Utaradit was supposed to enter, was so securely jammed down that it was impossible to prize it open with a penknife. On the other hand, the small door at the bottom of the box, which is usually used for taking out the letters, was left unlocked with the key in the lock—from both of which signs it was quite manifest that the confiding Siamese public had not yet learnt to entrust their letters to a Post Office. Several passers-by pointed out the red pillar to me with scarce concealed pride, and invited me to put my letters into it.

After breakfast I cleaned myself up and made ready to call on the Siamese Commissioner, to whom I had a letter of introduction. It turned out that I had not far to go, the Post Office being at his very gates. Moreover, we were more or less acquainted already, for, to my fearful horror, I found that we had been grazing our ponies in his compound all the morning, thereby moving a fat female slave to much wrath and indignation. The Commissioner, who seemed to bear no malice, was a tall, thin, fierce-looking gentleman, sadly afflicted with congestion of the liver. Of course he consulted me, and I as usual prescribed my only medicine, Vaseline. He ate a large chunk of this, and an hour or two afterwards came to me saying he felt much better. It had a good effect on his temper too, for he promised to help us to get boats and to dispose of our ponies—a feat he had declared impossible at our first interview. I gave him a shawl just to jog his memory, and in return I was besieged all day by his wives carrying presents of eggs, fruit, tobacco, etc.

For several days I noticed a youth loafing about in a wistful sort of way with a bundle of letters under his arm. I thought he had designs on my few remaining rags, and cautioned Judh Bir to keep his weathermost eye on him. Things reached a crisis when, one morning whilst I was dozing with one eye open, I saw him stealthily enter my hut. I rose and rebuked him with considerable severity, pointing out to him the heinousness of his offence in trying to rob the stranger and foreigner of his little all. He received my verbal castigation with the greatest humility, and murmured in a deprecatory voice that he was very sorry to intrude, and that he did not want to steal, but that this was the Post Office and he was the Pôstmaster! Mutual apologies and a fair division of the Post Office immediately made.

A small Chinese boy aged about three years came one day with his Siamese nurse to see me. She was suckling him as they came in, but my young gentleman, easing off for a minute and scrambling down from her lap, strode up to me, and in a loud and imperious voice said, "I am Chou Shesheen (Governor Shesheen); who are you?" A first-class little man, and likely to become an ornament to his race if he ever reaches maturity, the latter perhaps rather a problematical contingency, considering the mixed diet he indulged in. Whilst with me, in addition to the above-mentioned wholesome nutriment, he ate two plantains, and would have smoked half-a-dozen cigarettes if his nurse had not stopped him in his wild career. He probably chews betel-nut as well.

It is utterly hopeless trying to get any idea of distances from the natives; they have not the haziest idea of measurements of any sort, and their calculations are so sublimely regardless of even the elements of accuracy, that I have refrained from mentioning distances between places except when actually traversed by us. Here is an example of this inaccuracy. As we were leaving the village of Noi on our journey to Muang Nan, we met a bullock caravan just arriving from the latter place. I asked the gentleman in charge how many marches it was to Muang Nan, thinking, perhaps not unnaturally, that having that moment completed the journey, he would have a fairly accurate idea of the number of days he had been on the road. His answer was, "Four marches—(1) Ma Poung, (2) Tapa, (3) Mashote, (4) Muang Nan." These proved to be—1st march, 8½ miles; 2nd march, 14½ miles; 3rd march, 24 miles; and 4th march, about 68 miles; or a total of 115 miles—a distance which the best bullock ever created never did under ten days, I will bet my Sunday hat.

Again, on leaving Muang Nan I asked the Prince how many marches it was to Utaradit. He replied that it was four marches. After journeying 40 miles towards Utaradit, we again asked how many marches remained, and were calmly informed that there were eight more! In fact, each individual calculates the distance according to his own peculiar taste and fancy. We were many times put to hard straits for want of food, being misled by the benighted heathen into thinking that we should find a village and food at the end of our day's march. We could not carry much with us, and had therefore to be careful not to be away from villages for two days together.

We halted on Sundays generally, or rather on what we thought were Sundays, our almanac having melted into pulp during a thunderstorm; they proved to be Tuesdays eventually. Taking the Sunday at Tapa village as typical of our weekly halts, business commenced by thoroughly washing ourselves and our clothes; as an extra treat I had a shave too; then we gave the ponies an extra grooming and extra feeds, and made all repairs required in their gear. After breakfast large relays of visitors came to call on me, headed by the chief, a nice old gentleman, who presented me with a fowl (horrible moorgi). I scarcely have the assurance to look a chicken in the face now, considering the awful havoc Judh Bir and I have made in the ranks of his relations, to the fifth generation. We calculate that between us we have eaten 270 old and young during our journey!

One old fellow brought the whole of his family, about twelve strong, whom he exhibited with becoming pride. Amongst them were two very pretty girls, the best looking we had seen anywhere; but unfortunately, like every other woman in the land, the whole effect was spoilt by their black teeth and mouths. This is accounted an additional attraction amongst these people, and is attained by steadily chewing betel every hour of the day since they were old enough to chew a chawgum. I was led to suppose that I could marry one of the ladies for Rs. 50 or thereabouts. During the rest of the day we loafed and slept and ate as much as we could lay hands on, and wished every day was Sunday. Taking a Sunday rest is a thoroughly good principle to go upon, not on high religious grounds only, but also as a sound practical manœuvre. Sunday, I take it, is a day of rest and repair after the wear and tear of a week of work or pleasure. The nature of rest required by different natures varies considerably. To ram a wretched schoolboy down into a corner and make him learn collects and catechisms all day isn't the way to rest him; it only gives him a rooted aversion to Sundays and its accompanying evils. In practice we found that, without one day a week for rest and repair, our gear broke down, our pack animals got footsore, and we ourselves jaded, ill, and worn out.

Every male biped amongst the Siamese is obliged

to go through a course of the priesthood, *i.e.* he shaves his head, puts on yellow clothes, and learns to read and write. When he has served his time of probation, he either returns to his own profession or else becomes a permanent priest. This law has one good effect, viz. the elementary education of nearly the whole of the males in the kingdom. Every village has its priest-house and school, and it is in the compound alongside of these that the guest-house for travellers is generally situated. We often made our midday halts at these houses, much to the delight of the schoolboys, to whom our arrival and appearance was as good as a show. And we in return got a good deal of amusement out of watching them. The desultory way in which they do their lessons is quite gratifying to behold. There is probably only one horribly industrious boy, who is learning the alphabet or else how to count. He writes it all out on a long waxed board, using a stick for a pencil; he then sings aloud what he has written, at the top of his voice; then rubbing it out, he repeats the whole process over and over again. There is another little boy doing the same lesson, but he goes off and frequently relaxes his mind with a little cock-fighting in a corner.

The head master, with the majority of the boys and masters, is busily engaged in letting off a bamboo mine at one end of the compound. He (the head master) even condescends to cock-fighting now and again.

What an improving spectacle it would have been, in the old days at Clifton, to have seen our late revered head master, Dr. Percival, issuing forth in cap and gown, and, accompanied by a few choice spirits from the Sixth Form, to let off crackers in the quad, or facetiously to blow up the porter with a bamboo mine: this by way of recreation between two difficult passages in Homer!

On entering Siam proper from the Laos States, the difference in costume is at once apparent. Instead of following the graceful fashion of knotting the hair on the top of the head, as the Laos women do, the Siamese cut their hair quite short and leave it to bristle all over, like a hedgehog's back, men and women all alike. In the matter of garments, both sexes wear a loin-cloth tied like an Indian syce's, and perhaps a shawl over the shoulders. It is often only after the minutest examination that a casual stranger can tell a man from a woman. In Laos, on the contrary, the women wear lungis, or short petticoats, as in

Burmah, and their *tout ensemble* is certainly very fresh, clean, and pleasing.

A little incident illustrative of the doubtful advantage of having too many wives, occurred one day when we were in the Commissioner's compound at Utaradit. A small lady about four years old, one of the Commissioner's crowd of daughters, ordered a little slave boy to do something: the boy refused to do it, whereupon little miss fell on him tooth and nail, and gave him a very bad five minutes of it. Then both of them ran off howling to tell lies to their elders, concerning the extent and origin of the squabble. Unfortunately for them the first person they met was the dissipated youth, my friend the Commissioner's son. He with that promptness which distinguishes great minds, and with the utmost impartiality, immediately ordered them both to be flogged, and, seizing a good swishy cane, himself proceeded to chastise little missy very soundly, some one else at the same time officiating on the slave boy. This hubbub brought out all the mammas in a torrent of words and screams, and they all immediately setting upon one another, such a hammering and screaming and scratching was set going, that the original cause of the row got quite forgotten, and every one assaulted every one else with delightful impartiality; the dissipated youth, who with commendable foresight had early extracted himself from the *mêlée*, standing by clothed in his haughtiest air, and clearly congratulating himself that he was not such a low thing as a woman. Judh Bir and I sat on a rail and criticised.

After three months' incessant and rapid marching, we were rather a sorry-looking crew. It was impossible to buy anything to replace our breakages and losses, except cotton clothes at Kiang Tung, and a week sufficed to turn these to rags. My basin was stolen at Kiang Tung, and the one I bought to replace it, made of iron, of local manufacture, fell down and broke like pottery. After that I was obliged to wash in and eat out of the same vessel, to wit a very leaky sandwich box about 8 inches square by 3 inches deep. Our lantern went the way of all lanterns very soon after we started, so that, if we could not get our evening meal by daylight, we had to eat it by the dim, religious, evil-smelling, and smoky light afforded by a rag dipped in pig's fat and hung over the edge of a saucer. My costume at this period consisted of an ancient, much torn pair of breeches, a sleeping suit coat, and a Shan straw hat (Joe the pony having eaten my own); my sole remaining boots I wore only now and then for a treat, in fear and trembling lest the last few remaining stitches should give way. Judh Bir, my Goorka orderly, who had been by turns a Laos, a Shan, and a Chinaman, was now a pleasing mixture of all three, with a Chinaman's hat, a Shan's coat, and a Laos loin-cloth. Our food consisted of stewed fowl, green parrots, an occasional dove, and rice. Let me recommend the gourmand reader to try a fowl stewed with rice without any flavouring whatever if he wants to taste something really nasty: boiled dishcloths is a savoury dish in comparison. How we used to loathe the sight of that pot, and, though we were ravenously hungry, how very little of it could we manage to swallow! At large towns pork and beef are procurable, generally terrifically tough. Our drink was a nauseous mixture of goor (coarse sugar) and water, taken hot, for we were afraid to drink unboiled water. To this stage of depravity we fell by degrees: from Indian tea we descended to cheap China green tea at about threepence a pound, and my cook-boy keeping us in ignorance when that was finished, we went on drinking goor and water for several days without missing the tea from it. So we continued the fraud:

it looked like tea, and Judh Bir assured me it was considered most nourishing. I think it must have been, for, in spite of our meagre fare and hard work, we both kept fit and strong and did not lose much weight. There is no milk or butter throughout the land, and the only vegetables we came across were onions and chillies; nor did we see a single sheep or goat. Fish are abundant in all the rivers, but we were very unlucky, generally getting very bony ones.

CHAPTER VI.

UTARADIT BY BOAT TO BANGKOK.

Leave Utaradit—Parting with Joe and Chang—Enjoy rest—The Me Nan River—Boatmen—Scarcity of game—Phitsanalok—Junction of Me Nioum and Me Nan Rivers—Remote tribes more cordial—Denounce hectoring of natives—The man of hats — Bangkok — Description of Siamese — Cremation — Siamese policy—British influence at Bangkok preponderates—Chinese, their enterprise—Royal Horse Guards on parade—Siamese police—Taxes innumerable—The bamboo and its uses—Gambling—Siam worst country for sport—Climate—Leave Bangkok for Singapore—Parting with Ananias.

AFTER a great deal of trouble we managed on April 28th to engage a boat, to take us down the Me Nan River to Bangkok. It had been our intention to cross Central Siam to Rahang, and there take boat to Bangkok; but the season was far advanced, and the rains had set in regularly, making land travelling not only very difficult, but with pack ponies almost impossible. We also entered into an agreement for the transport by raft of our four ponies, thinking that there would be a good market for them in Bangkok; but at the last moment it was discovered that there was not sufficient water in the river to float so heavy a load, and we had reluctantly to leave them behind. Rather than hand them over to the tender mercies of the Siamese, we hired a couple of men, and sent them to Dr. Cheek at Zimmé; but I imagine they were stolen on the road, for I have never heard yet that they reached Dr. Cheek. The parting between Joe and I was most affecting; he ran down to the shore ninnying quite sadly as we rowed away. A right tight little fellow, a friend and companion for months which seemed like years; and though he vexed my soul very often, yet he was always so jolly and merry over it, that I could never be really angry with him. I should like to have brought him home with me, but that was out of the question. May he have fallen into kind hands! Chang, with his usual *sangfroid*, was fast asleep on the ashes of last night's fire, and as usual objected to getting up early, his daily custom being to rise a couple of hours after we started, and then tracking us out, to catch us up at our midday halting-place. We had to carry him into the boat, much to his disgust: once there he was as happy as possible, and went to sleep for three days and nights on end, only waking to eat occasionally. We lost him too, a few days later, for he jumped on shore at one of the villages we stopped at, without being noticed; and when his loss was discovered, it was too late to go back. A faithful old dog, who had followed us throughout our long journey, and whose very presence in our bivouac was enough to keep all suspicious characters at a safe distance. He was a most peculiar-looking dog, as hairless as a scalded pig; he would have been a great curiosity at home.

Before starting we discharged our last remaining Shan boy, "Combien," a smart youth, with the finest pair of legs in Asia. He was never tired or footsore, though he had some stiffish work, always having to go off and forage for food at the end of our long daily marches. I sent him across with the ponies to Dr. Cheek, but I suppose the temptation of walking off with them *en route* was too great to resist.

The scenery down the river was very beautiful, the stream winding through thick forests, with picturesque villages nestling in their foliage. All the low-lying banks were used for tobacco cultivation, which, with small patches of rice land here and there, were all the crops we saw. We found lolling about in a comfortable boat an unspeakable luxury after our hundreds of miles of trudge, trudge, trudge. No more anxieties about grass and water for the ponies; no more weary searches for food when we were longing only for sleep and rest; no more nights in the soaking dew and bitter cold of the Shan hills; no more exasperating tracking out of stray ponies in the chill dawn. All was now rest, and that abiding peace which only those who have roughed it in the wild places of the earth can fully appreciate. Judh Bir and Ananias, poor fellows, who by choice had footed the whole of that long march, simply lay like logs and revelled in the luxury of twenty-two hours' sleep per diem. Mine was bodily ease only, for I was anxious to roughly survey this magnificent Me Nan River, which seemed to have escaped the notice of most previous travellers; and therefore every ten minutes throughout the day, and a greater portion of the night, I took soundings and angles, and wrote reams of notes which I have by me, but they are of no interest to the general reader.

Going with the current, I calculated our rate was about 3½ miles an hour. The first large place we passed was Muang Bechai, on the second day, a town like all those in Lower Siam, partly on land and partly on the river. Here we met the first detachment of regular soldiers that we had seen in the country. They were a very ordinary-looking crowd, dressed in blue cotton uniform with white facings. Their rifles, Tower-marked muzzle-loaders, were piled in a heap on the ground, and were so covered with rust as to be practically useless. They wore white European helmets.

The few glimpses we could get of the surrounding country showed an immense forest-covered plain, with a low line of hills running parallel to the river, and varying from twenty miles to five miles east of its course. The river has the most ridiculously winding course, at one minute running due south, and the next due north, and then round to the east or west.

The Me Nan River rises in the range of mountains which skirt the south bank of the Me Kong (or Cambodia) River, in about lat. 19° 41′ N., and long. 100° 45′ E. Its approximate length is 430 miles, *i.e.* to the point where the Me Ping joins it at Paknampho. Onwards the two rivers take the name of Menam. Its general direction is from north to south, and there are no exaggerated bends to the east or west as in the Me Kong River; but looking at it from a minuter point of view, it will be found that its course is very tortuous indeed. Except in two portions—first, near its source where it is flowing through low hills, and again when it bursts through the chain of hills south of Muang Sa—it runs entirely through the deep clay soil of a country sloping imperceptibly towards the Gulf of Siam. The current is therefore, except at the numerous gentle rapids, very slight.

Below Utaradit it becomes so winding that often for a mile or so the river will be running due north, *i.e.* exactly in the opposite direction to its true course. The Menam is navigable as far up as Utaradit, 230 miles above, for Paknampho, for the largest river-boats and small steam launches during the rainy season, and for ordinary boats drawing 2 ft. of water, throughout the year. From Utaradit, up as high as Muang Phak (Ta Phak), the river is navigable for small boats during the greater part of the year. Above that point come shallows and rapids, quite impassable for anything but unloaded canoes. To the north of the rapids the river again becomes navigable for river-boats for about sixty miles.

From Utaradit southwards there is a very large and prosperous trade in tobacco, the banks in all low-lying parts being lined with tobacco fields. Rice too, to some extent, is carried down to Bangkok, but not on such a large scale as down the Me Ping River. The boats on the return voyage bring back cheap English cotton goods, flannel, kerosene oil, ironmongery, and odds and ends and kickshaws.

On the 28th of April we passed during the day 105 boats either moored or moving up stream; on the 29th, 209 boats. The great majority are in the tobacco trade. Though the river is not fordable for men, the current is very slow; but in many places it is fordable for elephants.

Early on the third day of our voyage, we passed a European going up stream in a boat, the first white face we had seen for ages. I was so taken aback, that by the time I had hulloaed to him, we had shot past each other, and were out of hail. He probably did not recognise me as a European, for I was a most villanous-looking ruffian dressed in Shan clothes. It was being thus passed without a sign of recognition that made me think of borrowing a small-looking glass from the boatman. I am not very beautiful at the best of times, but I don't remember, in all my wanderings, ever having met such an unmitigated cutthroat as that looking-glass showed me. A cross breed between a German music master and a broken-down Italian organ-grinder, would be a gentleman of the first water beside what I was. By the way, can my musical friends explain why musical genius and a rooted aversion to visiting the hairdresser generally go hand in glove? After a large experience of many nations I have come to the conclusion that the Britisher, and more especially the British soldier-officer, is the cleanest and best groomed man on earth. The worst, excepting perhaps Usbegs and such like people who never wash, is the German musical genius. The Siamese are openly, and even aggressively, clean; for men, women, and children bathe three or four times a day, all in "a state of adorable nature," as Monsieur deftly puts it.

We had pelting rain for the greater part of most days, and glad we were to be able to creep into our snug little cabin, and congratulate ourselves that we were not struggling across country with our poor old baggage tats. The nights were very close and muggy, and mosquitoes swarmed around us.

The boatmen are famous fellows for work: they

row all day, only knocking off for meals; after supper do three hours more, starting again at dawn. The great preponderance of women is very remarkable, more so than in Laos. One sees three women to one man, and all doing men's work, rowing boats, looking after cattle, carrying water (two kerosine tins on a pole banghy-wise). Next in number to the women come the Chinamen, who compose apparently the majority of inhabitants in the larger places; they have each two or three Siamese wives. We have seen no Chinese women south of Kuang Tung. All the boatmen are very skilful in sculling along their little boats and keeping their heads straight. This seems to be done by dwelling a little on the end of the stroke, but is done so neatly as to be imperceptible. All row standing, and with their faces to the bow.

Game of all sorts was singularly scarce. We only saw one flight of teal during the whole of our river journey; a few Imperial pigeons were all we bagged. For something to do, and also to help to clear the world of monsters, we used to practise flying shots at the alligators we passed, and killed five or six of them. The boatmen used to cut out their hearts and hang them up in the bow of the boat, partly for luck and partly to scare away any evil-disposed spirits that might be cruising around at night.

On the evening of April 30th we reached Phitsanalok, a large and comparatively important town.

Most of the people seem to be engaged in tobacco cultivation. We saw no cattle, and could get no meat except pork. The banks are too high, and the slope of the river too slight, to allow of much irrigation. We passed a boatful of very large fish of every description just caught in a large net. We bought a young salmon for three pice, the larger ones being three annas each.

We had heavy rain here; the thermometer before had been 90° to 94° at midday and 77° at night; after rain falling, it fell to 88° and 71°.

Phitsanalok is a long thin place on the left bank of the River Me Nan. The houses lie in the midst of thick foliage, and are closely packed. There were about 200 boats here, mostly inhabited, besides many floating huts. We saw a great many Chinamen here, and all well to do; the best houses, the largest boats, the fattest pigs, all belonging to Chinamen. They all have harems of Siamese women.

Most of the bazaar shops are in the boats, only a

few stalls on the top of the bank. There were Chinese liquor-shops, and gambling houses abound as at Utaradit. There are no bridges the whole length of the river. We saw no game with the exception of one small flight of teal.

The country generally is open thin forest, with high reed grass thick in parts and quite level. There are a great number of mango-trees growing wild on the banks, and we got great quantities of mangoes very cheap—a large basket for three annas. To see Judh Bir and Ananias stowing them away made my stomach ache. I sat at my end of the boat and croaked at them: "You will both die of cholera as sure as eggs is eggs;" but they only laughed, and laid on with renewed vigour.

On the night of May 3rd we passed the junction of the Me Nioum and Me Nan Rivers. As it will be remembered, we had followed the former for about 100 miles from its source, in an earlier part of our journey. It had been running parallel to us all along; it is one of the three great rivers which drain the central portion of Siam from its northern borders to the sea. Our boatman told us that it was as large and navigable as the Me Nan which we were descending.

Next day we reached Päknampho, on 4th of May, a large and important town at the junction of the Me Ping (the Zimmé) River with the Me Nan.

The Me Ping rushes in with great force, but looks small and insignificant, more like a large mill-stream than the end of a big river. Of the two the Me Nan is larger, deeper, and more navigable. It is strange that it is not better known and more used. We saw no signs of irrigation cuts off the river.

Paknampho is built along either banks of both rivers, the town being nearly entirely confined to the river banks either on land or floating huts. There is a post office as well as a telegraph office here, the main telegraph line to Zimmé crossing the river below.

In the lower reaches of the river we found the greatest difficulty in getting the bare necessities of life in the way of food. We were closing down on the regions of civilization and the tracks of the inevitable white man. Above, in the wild countries, where few if any white men had penetrated before us, we met with nothing but kindness and hospitality, and I trust most sincerely we never did anything to make the paths of our successors thorny. Certainly we made a point of always making ourselves popular with our hosts, and I really hope succeeded. I can't write too strongly against the blustering, bullying cad of an Englishman (or other foreigner), who, passing through a virgin country, prostitutes and disgraces the name and reputation of the white man. If the first white man a barbarian sees and meets is a hectoring bully, the impression is firmly imbedded in his mind that all white men are like the first of that race he has had the misfortune to meet. Bullying and hectoring seem to be indulged in mostly by quite the most contemptible of our race. A man who is like a tame cat in his dealings with his white fellow-creatures takes a delight in lording it over any weaker vessels that he may find amongst weaker nations. Of course there are times when the temper of the best of men, perhaps sorely tried by hunger and privations, will break out a little, under excessive provocation. That happens once in a way and is over and done for, whilst the weak man blusters with every one he thinks will stand it from him. It is difficult to explain why, but certainly it is impossible not to notice the degrading effect Western civilization has on Orientals. Look at the Bengali Babu, the highest intellectual outcome of our enlightened rule; is it possible in any nation to find such a contemptible character? A quantity of half-digested Western notions, congealed together in a mass of inert fat, neither a physical nor an intellectual success, whose sole redeeming point is a sort of selfish industry, which, by the way, was his before we ever knew him. So in Siam, up north, away from civilization; it is impossible to imagine a more genial, hospitable, and thoroughly pleasant race to travel amongst. Down south there is no geniality, no hospitality; a surly, sulky people, not fit to hold a candle to their northern brethren. No doubt it is our mission to colonize and civilize; but somehow we don't go the right way about it—too much of "the Bible in one hand and a six shooter in the other" kind of policy perhaps.

As we progressed, the river constantly split up into many channels, which rejoined again lower down. Many large and flourishing towns were passed; in fact during the last two days before reaching Bangkok both banks of the river were lined with an almost continuous succession of houses.

The man of Siam is essentially a man of hats—hats manifold of all sorts, sizes, and shapes, ranging from Mr. Christie's felt billycock down to the grass-thatched roof of local manufacture. No man or woman, however poor they may be, is without a hat of some description, though the rest of their costume may consist only of a string tied round the waist. The captain of my boat, for instance, wore by turns two very elegant felt hats, one white and the other brown; both made by Mr. Christie of London, each having cost at least Rs. 6. The rest of his attire being a small loin-cloth, the *tout ensemble* was very chaste and pleasing. The chimney-pot' hat of my nation was the only hat known to civilized man which was not represented. Another form of dandyism is the cultivation of the finger-nails to quite an appalling length. I measured one gentleman's middle finger-nail, and found it 2¼ inches long (this is not a fable). This eminently satisfactory result can of course only be obtained after months, perhaps years, of careful cultivation, during which period sufficient soil for a fair-sized cabbage garden is gradually accumulated.

We reached Bangkok on May 9th, having been twelve days making the river voyage from Utaradit. We rowed straight to the British Consulate, which is situated on the water's edge, to get letters and news. Mr. E. B. Gould, who was kindness and hospitality personified, very kindly offered to put us up. I shall never quite forget that first most delicious bottle of beer and tempting dinner after feeding for months on garbage, and drinking nothing but the goor* and water of affliction. To hear my native tongue again, the Consul's improving conversation, and the Doctor's amusing stories really was too jolly for words. Siam certainly must agree with the white man, for I am sure no country could produce better fellows than Mr. Gould, Dr. Cheek, and half-a-dozen others of the real right sort. I feel quite inclined to go and be a General in the Siamese Army, though perhaps on second thoughts I had better not after that fiery article of mine in the *Bombay Gazette.*† The King would perhaps cut off my head, or qualify me for the charge of two or three hundred of his Queens.

The people of Siam are in character inferior to the Laos. The men drink, gamble, and sleep; all the work, except ploughing, being done by women. As an instance of the different code of morals, it may be mentioned that whereas in Laos you may turn your elephant, buffaloes, ponies adrift to graze, and they are as safe as in a stable, in Siam they would be

* Coarse sugar.

† Pitching into something that did not seem fair play to me.

immediately stolen. The penalty for theft in both alike is death—in Laos a stern reality, in Siam a fiction. It sounds rather a bloody code, and is so in theory, but in practice the very severity of the law is its own salvation, and no man breaks it. Theft may be considered an unknown crime in Laos. Another form of theft, and a most glaring and impudent one, is the theft of hats off the heads of people as they drive past. The ponies are very small, and the carriages the same, so that a man running up from behind can snatch off your hat, and dart down a by-street before you can pull up. There is not much competition for my hat, I notice, and I do not intend to get a new one here. The whole trade is in the hands of Chinamen, and one cannot sufficiently admire the admirable working qualities of this race. They turn their hands to anything and everything, and their diligence and industry is wonderful. One Chinaman's work is considered equal to that of four Siamese. The Siamese make very indifferent servants, and have no knowledge of cookery.

As in Laos, the Siamese cremate their dead except in cases of violent death. We visited the public cremating ground, and a more revolting spectacle it would be difficult to imagine.

The place is in the heart of the city, surrounded by a high wall. On entering, two or three corpses, on brick fire rests, are seen opposite, slowly burning. Around are several long open sheds. In these were piled up hundreds of boxes of all sorts and sizes, looking like the brickyard of any dry goods man's store. I asked what they were, thinking they were merely old wood used in cremating. To my horror the gentleman answered, they were full of corpses in various states of decomposition. People bring them here and store them until they have money enough to burn them. Sometimes this is never achieved, as one or two shattered old boxes, with skeletons dropping out of them, sufficiently testified. Of course the stench was overpowering. But this was not the worst. If a prisoner dies and has no friends to burn him, his body is thrown out into a brick-yard made for the purpose, and there left for the vultures to consume.

In this yard were the remains of many hundred corpses, all presenting the most sickening spectacle.

As we entered, the vultures flapped lazily to one side, and a little child ran laughing up to us and asked for bucksheesh, and on looking round we saw other children playing about utterly oblivious to the awful scene around them. Such is the effect of habit on humanity. A familiarity with vice, crime, or barbarity deadens the better feelings, and lowers us to the level of the beasts. Such is the poor man's and the criminal's funeral.

From here we went to the King's relation's funeral, and the contrast was tremendous. There, an enormous wat, or building covered with gold, had been raised over the body; it was a spacious building covering a couple of acres of ground, the structure erected temporarily, and which will be pulled down when the ceremony is completed. The King himself, with all his army and nobles, was present.

The kingdom of Siam forms the greater portion of the Indo-Chinese Peninsula, and lies between Burmah and the French possessions of Annam and Tonquin. It is an independent country, governed by a despotic monarch, which has of late years drawn to itself the attention of the great Western Powers by its apparently sincere endeavours to raise itself to the level of Western civilization.

How far these endeavours have succeeded will be seen later; at present the chief result seems to have been to attract the unwelcome attentions of one if not both of its two great and powerful neighbours, to each of whom the gentle flutterings of its monarch towards civilization has made apparent the golden future in store for that nation which shall bring Siam under its civilizing power.

A country inhabited by a docile and easily governed race, drained by great and navigable rivers which flow through almost inexhaustible teak forests, and immense tracts of rice and tobacco—a country having a climate salubrious when compared with that of other Eastern lands, and a soil capable of raising the richest crops, with its sapphire and ruby mines, iron and copper, silver and coal—it bids fair to become a very Eldorado to that enterprising and energetic nation which is bold enough to take it.

The Siamese policy is to pose as the "promising child" of the East, the plucky little kingdom which is struggling far ahead of its neighbours out of the black slough of barbarity. That extremely infectious and unwholesome disease called love of notoriety, for which the only soothing medicine is a "newspaper notice," has reached this far-away spot. The King of Siam is as pleased or otherwise with a newspaper paragraph concerning himself as any lady of the *corps de ballet.*

The whole of his civilization is really a very hollow sham, got up especially for newspaper notices, and through the newspapers making a bid for European notoriety. We are quite surprised when we first hear that the King of Siam has an army, dressed and equipped like Europeans, and officered by European officers, a small navy of English-built men-of-war, a police force, postal and telegraph services, and a local coinage; an English chaplain, barrister, and doctor on his personal staff. But when we come to examine more closely these signs of civilization, we find that the army is a mere rabble, very inefficient, and utterly unfit to cope with the worst regular troops in Asia; the ships of the navy so completely rotten that it is only with constant tinkering that they are prevented from sinking at their moorings. The police force, like the rest, is an agreeable farce got up for the edification of foreign newswriters. The postal arrangements are most dilatory and unsafe. And finally we see the chaplain, barrister, and doctor drawing their pay (much in arrears) and helping to swell the magnificent fraud.

I think the King of Siam and his more enlightened advisers are fully aware that their kingdom exists only on sufferance. They fully understand that their country is a Naboth's vineyard to one great nation, the French: and another, the English, though not desirous itself of annexing Siam, would rather do so than see it in the hands of the French. The King, when asked, "Are you not afraid of these two powerful neighbours who are threatening you on either side? Why do you not increase your army and navy, and import more European officers to increase their efficiency?" replies quite candidly, "If I was to turn every man in my kingdom into a soldier and arm them with the best of weapons, even then I could not hope to cope with either of these great Western nations: why therefore should I spend money on a useless pageantry?".

This gives the King's whole policy in a nutshell—a policy played with such success by small and comparatively weak nations constantly throughout the history of the world. It is a policy which, by discreetly playing off one powerful neighbour against another, secures a safety and independence for the weaker State which the largest armaments it could raise would be unable to procure for it. As Switzerland is to Germany, Austria, and France; as Belgium is to Germany, France, and England,—so is Siam to

England, France, and China in the East. This the King of Siam has been sharp enough to see. He looks on the English as the most powerful nation in the East, the most powerful friend, and the most powerful enemy. From his standpoint, that of a king who lives on sufferance, his natural leanings are therefore decidedly Britishwards, perhaps from inclination, more probably from policy. We can understand it being difficult to regard with unmixed friendship a comparatively omnipotent neighbour at whose tender mercy one's country lies.

A visit to Bangkok at once proclaims to the traveller the preponderance of British influence. Half the European residents are English; shopmen have their signboards painted in English; English is the language of the Telegraph Department; and the Siamese postage stamps and coinage have English inscriptions. The public buildings have their names engraved in English above the portals. In fact, to the casual observer, Bangkok appears as much English as Aden. From a British point of view these proclivities are most encouraging.

As for the French, by their aggressive policy in Cambodia and Annam they have, temporarily at least, completely ruined their own prospects in Siam.

At first the King of Siam welcomed the advent of a rival Western nation in Cochin China as a possible ally against the English, whose earlier conquests in Burmah and the Malay Peninsula were sufficient to raise a feeling of insecurity and distrust. The French, with inexcusable want of foresight, failed to grasp the situation. Instead of at once assuming the *rôle* of a great protecting Power, and thereby making French influence paramount at Bangkok, they proceeded to rob the King of Siam of part of his kingdom, with the natural result of throwing him into the arms of the English.

In making this comparison it must not, however, be forgotten that though at this moment English customs and English counsels predominate, yet the Siamese, with excusable forethought, still keep on such a footing with the French, that, practising on the well-known rivalry between the two nations, they could at once summon them to their aid if offered violence by England. To the English the King says, "Hands off, or I shall call in the French;" and to the French, "Don't try me too far, or I shall get the English to intervene." Practising this policy, he hopes to live in peace and happiness, troubled by no foreign cares, unburdened with an army or navy—

a typical Eastern monarch (in a swallow-tailed coat and top hat), with his 800 wives and plenty of loose cash to jingle in his pocket.

The Chinese question, though dwarfed in the Siamese mind before the more imminent and deadly dangers which threaten their country from east and west, is nevertheless likely in the long run to become the greatest source of disquietude to them. It at once strikes a stranger in Bangkok, and also in a gradually diminishing degree as he moves northward, what an enormous hold the Chinese have on the country. Apparently the whole business and commerce of the country is in the hands of the Chinese; and we may look to this hardy and industrious race for the further development of its resources. The Siamese themselves seem to have nothing higher than a twopenny-halfpenny idea of commerce; they do no trade on any large scale as far as I could see. Perhaps this is not altogether from inaptitude, but it is possible that their commercial aspirations have been nipped in the bud by the frost of oppression. No ordinary man dare appear rich, for fear of falling a prey to the local vulture who calls himself a Prince, and wears violet-coloured silk stockings and a black "bowler" hat.

This is all very prosy and dry, and I for one am quite sick of it; let us return to the realms of comedy, let us look at the Siamese Army.

A parade is ordered of the Royal Horse Guards, numbering sixty troopers in all, mounted for the most part on large, straggly-looking Walers, with a few twelve-hand Burmese ponies thrown in by way of contrast. Let us drop in and criticize them in a friendly way. The first person to appear on the parade-ground is a solitary horseman: he is clad more or less like an English Life Guardsman, but has left his boots at home, apparently the more effectually to exhibit a very nice pair of blue stockings with white toes. On closer inspection he proves to be the trumpeter, about to summon his brave comrades to the field of action. Now whether he was suddenly fired with martial ardour at the sight of two foreigners, or what, has never been ascertained, but at any rate he pulled up, and, with the utmost recklessness, commenced blowing on his instrument the local "to boots and saddles." Before two notes of the clarion trumpet had rung on the still air our impetuous friend was lying on the broad of his back in the middle of the road, with his fiery steed standing by and looking down on him with rather a deprecatory air. During the rest of the manœuvres our gallant friend the trumpeter, when the stern call of duty required that he should blow a "call," invariably dismounted and handed over his steed to a pal in the crowd to hold whilst he performed.

Shortly after, the main body of the Royal Horse Guards arrived, and a very dashing-looking set of fellows they were, each and all sitting their horses like Centaurs, so long as no disturbing influences were brought to bear on them. The first disturbing influence occurred all too soon: it was the "Royal Salute," which was fired on the approach of the King. The first gun was the signal for those Royal Horse Guardsmen who were discreetly minded immediately to dismount and hold their horses; and those who were not so minded were instantly and violently hurled to the ground by their proud coursers.

In the infantry, the Siamese officers furnished the ludicrous element to the parade. All the officers, we were told, were Princes of high rank: there seemed to be about one Prince to every six men, though of course this is hardly a matter of astonishment when we consider that off and on there are 800 Queens. They (the Princes) arrived in driblets, some fully equipped, some dressed in a tunic dhoti and lavender-coloured stockings, and some in the mufti of their nation. The latter two parties changed into the imposing uniform of their regiment on and about the parade. One old gentleman, whose servant had arrived before him with his uniform, might be seen struggling into a pair of gold-laced trousers on the parade-ground, at the same time exhorting his men with great vigour to "order arms," "pile arms," etc. During off moments in the course of the manœuvres the army falls out and goes to an outdoor theatre close by, on the boards of which a seemingly never-ending play is kept going for the benefit of the licentious soldiery.

The police force is under the command of an Englishman who rejoices in the modest Siamese name of Hluang Rathyadbipatabanija. Three European and five Siamese inspectors assist him to support this title. The force is supposed to consist of about 300 men, a large majority of whom are old and decrepid. The uniform consists of a dark blue cotton coat and trousers, encircled by a black belt furnished with the orthodox truncheon; a sou'-westerish-looking solah topee, covered with black oilskin, completes the outfit. The general effect is distinctly ludicrous, and I seriously annoyed several guardians of the peace by falling into dangerously apoplectic fits of laughter when I suddenly encountered one of these fossils at a sharp corner of the street.

There is a tax on almost everything, down to fish-hooks and the fish caught with them. These taxes are farmed out almost entirely to Chinamen, which means that the Chinaman pays down a lump sum to the Treasury and then proceeds to squeeze double that sum out of the people. Indeed, one case came to our notice in which a Chinaman bought the tax on bamboos for Rs. 6000, and succeeded in wringing Rs. 65,000 out of the people! This was a tax on the bamboo, which grows like a weed all over Siam, and is the staff of life to the natives.

The gentleman who introduced this form of torture certainly deserves the sincerest thanks of the Treasury.

The bamboo is certainly the staff of life to the forester. Its uses are almost numberless. I have come across it in the following forms. My elephant's pad and howdahs are made of it.

By cutting a good thick bamboo, so that one of the rims comes at the bottom, an excellent water-bucket is formed.

In wild villages the whole house is built of bamboo, walls and roofs all being of bamboo flattened out into planks.

Strips of bamboo are used instead of ropes, and act admirably.

The elephant and bullock bells are of bamboo.

One carries no tent poles, each camp affording its own bamboos, light, strong, and cut down with two blows of a "dah;" tent pegs also.

The leaf is a nutritious, healthy food for horses and mules; they eat it greedily. The strippings of your tent-poles feed your horses. For horse bedding this is also used.

At each halting-place the Chinese and Shans run up in a few minutes strong pens for their pack animals, all of bamboo—uprights, bars, and fastenings. All these and many more are the uses of the bamboo in the forest, besides the numerous uses it is put to in civilized parts by skilled workmen.

As every one knows, it is almost impossible in the Siamese climate to destroy a clump of bamboos. Cut them down, dig them up by the roots, burn them, do anything you like, and before the next rains are half-way through, your clump will have sprouted up again. It speaks volumes for the docility of the people, that the Chinaman, a foreigner, can, without any assistance, active or passive, from the police or magistrates, go round and collect his taxes himself. Perhaps docility is hardly the word to give to this trait in their character—it is more nearly apathy, the outcome of generations of tyranny on a race of slaves.

The greatest source of revenue is, we heard, derived from gambling-house licences. In Bangkok every third house in the city is a gambling-house, the other two being a pawnbroker's and a brothel.

Gambling is universal amongst all classes, men and women, and every species is resorted to. The more sporting confine themselves to cock-fighting, fish-fighting, and cockchafer-fighting. The latter two are novel.

The fish-fighting is a pretty sight, the little fellows changing colour constantly, charging and tearing each other's fins with the greatest ferocity.

When one of the belligerents has had enough of it he turns a leaden colour, and flees round and round the tank followed by his victorious friend.

Cockchafer-fighting is a very curious sight. I came across a Chinaman choosing a good pair out of a lot which a girl was carrying round for sale.

The two pugilists were put into a round tin basin, which had two cross sticks wedged in across the top. On the cross was placed a small box with an entrance to it. The cockchafer that drove his opponent into this box was considered the victor.

They both required a good deal of poking up, and the sport rather palled on one after an hour or two.

The post office is a new toy of the King's, and can hardly be considered a really efficient service. The opening of the local postal service in Bangkok was a tremendous success, the lower classes at once discovering a Heaven-sent method of most effectually and securely annoying their rulers. Consequently every man of any position or mark was daily assailed by bundles of anonymous post-cards and letters, each and all couched in the most opprobrious terms which envy and malice combined, with a feeling of safety from discovery, could dictate. The eminent recipients of these missives very naturally conceived a deadly hatred against the innovator of their woes, the Postal Department, and there is no doubt that its days would have been numbered then and there with a nation more prompt in action. Delay fortunately in this case brought relief, for the writers finding their attacks did no harm to any one else, and themselves no good, gradually ceased from troubling, and the Postal Department pursues the even tenor of its way.

I think Siam may be considered one of the worst countries in the East from a sporting point of view. We travelled over some 1800 miles of country; sometimes through dense hilly forest, sometimes across open level grassy plains, and sometimes by boat along magnificent rivers, and yet we saw no game or even tracks of any game. A hare was the largest wild beast we came across, and only one of him; we also had the good fortune to encounter one partridge and two bush quail. Finally, during a 500-mile river journey we saw only one solitary flight of teal. This seems strange, for the greater part of our journey was through a virgin country which had never been shot over, and as a rule in such countries animal life, both sporting and otherwise, abounds. Before starting I had visions of rhinoceros simply jostling each other and asking to be shot; tigers and leopards in such numbers that I should get quite *blasé* about shooting anything under 13 ft. in length; and as for all the smaller kinds of game, both fourfooted and winged, that they would sit about in large numbers on the muzzle of my gun, all competing for the pleasure of supplying my cook with succulent morsels. To tackle all this game, we took a large magazine of firearms and enough ammunition to assault a town with. It can easily be imagined then how gruesome we felt after these high hopes having to live for days together on green parrots, with an occasional dove thrown in for a luxury. The craft and subtlety with which Judh Bir used to stalk a dove would have been quite amusing, if I had not been in an agony of fear lest he should miss it and leave me dinnerless. He very seldom did, I must say, for he used to crawl on the pit of his stomach till he got the gun well up against his victim, and then pulled the trigger.

In some parts the Imperial pigeon, a magnificent bird weighing as much as an Indian fowl, was fairly plentiful, but his skin was as thick as a dogskin glove, and nothing under a Gatling gun would bring him down.

Taken as a whole the climate of Siam may be considered decidedly good for an Eastern country. Throughout the hottest weather, *i.e.* in March, April, and May, we marched all day; and though it could hardly be called pleasant, yet there was no serious hardship in doing so. Except in Bangkok, the nights were cool and refreshing everywhere; and save on the rivers, mosquitoes and sandflies wonderfully scarce. The rains, which last from April to September or October, are not unhealthy, but after that, to the end of December, is the sickly season caused by the drying up of the country. The healthiest months are January, February, and March.

After a week's stay at Bangkok in Mr. Gould's hospitable house, we got a passage in a horrid little ship, and started for Singapore. I have travelled in all sorts of ships, from the lordly "Trooper" down to a collier in the Red Sea, but I never was quite so uncomfortable as I was on that vessel. Pigs I don't mind, nor sheep, nor camels, but I do object to being unceremoniously kicked out of bed by a crowd of cockchafers; my own private bunk too, and for which I had paid 50 dollars. We must have been carrying a cargo of sugar, I think, and there wasn't enough of it for all of them. The run to Singapore takes a couple of days. There we put up at the Hôtel de l'Europe, one of the worst and dearest anywhere in the East. I probably should not make that last remark if I thereby thought I should injure the custom of the hotel; I couldn't do that though, for there is no rival hotel, and the traveller must perforce, be it good or be it bad, go to this one. Mr. Sugden, of the Borneo Company, very kindly put me up for the club, which I entered with a good deal of trepidation, for I certainly was a most disreputable-looking object, in spite of some very elegant clothes I had bought at a marine pawnbroker's at Bangkok. The hall porter manifestly viewed me with suspicion, and trembled for the portable plate of the club. I forget its name, but it is a most comfortable and hospitable one, and the short drinks are beyond all praise. If I might place one before another, my verdict is in favour of the whisky cocktail.

My habiliments certainly must have been most uncouth, as was brought home to me very forcibly by my landlord at the hotel, himself most accurately attired in the best fitting of clothes. After dinner I was sitting outside smoking, and thinking how jolly the stars looked, and how exceedingly glad I was to be well on my way home; and after the manner of subalterns rather wondering if a certain pair of blue eyes was also gazing at the stars, or whether, on the contrary, they were gazing fondly on the hated rival, when the landlord strolled up and began to talk to me. He evidently had grave doubts about my ability to square his account, and came to pump me accordingly, I suppose. These I managed to quell, and then he made the remark about my outer man, which is alluded to above. Mentioning a tight-rope performance that was then in progress at the Town Hall close by, he said, "I don't think they would let you in as you are, but if I lend you an old coat I am sure they would admit you into the gallery!"

At Singapore we parted company with Ananias, who was to go by a separate ship to Moulmein, his home. Since our return to civilized parts, I had seen little or nothing of Ananias, his time being occupied in riotousness and drunkenness, to make up for months of enforced abstinence. He wasn't a bad fellow on the whole, and had certainly shown wonderful staying powers. To my everlasting credit be it related that I never whacked him once, though at times he had driven me to the verge of desperation.

Judh Bir and I embarked on a ship with a Chinese name, and a captain who led us to believe that he was a great favourite with the ladies. However, in spite of these drawbacks, we reached Calcutta quite safely and our long journey was over.

In conclusion, I should like to apologise to any stray individual who has been kind enough to struggle through this book, for having afflicted a long-suffering public with it at all. It wasn't my fault in the least—I was egged on and intimidated into writing it by my old governor, whom I hereby deliberately hand over to the popular fury.

APPENDIX.

HINTS TO TRAVELLERS IN SIAM.

SIAM may be briefly described as a country covered with immense forests and divided longitudinally by four large and navigable rivers. The northern and western portions are covered by masses of forest-clad hills, and these tail off into the plains of the eastern and southern parts.

For the traveller by land there are five means of transport available, viz. by hired elephants, bullocks, coolies or carts, or by purchased mules and ponies. The most usual form of transport used by travellers in Siam is the elephant. It has many advantages and several disadvantages. The former are, its capacity for pushing its way through the densest jungle, fording rivers impassable for other animals, requiring no grain and finding all its grazing off the forest boughs; it can also be quickly and easily loaded and unloaded. The disadvantages are its slowness, its timidity and proneness to panic, especially at the sight of a horse, and the smallness of its howdah, which only admits of a very small load in actual bulk being carried.

In favour of bullock carriage I know nothing except that large numbers of bullocks are easily hired. Against them there is every objection; they are very slow, easily stampeded when loaded or otherwise, require grain, and half the day has to be wasted whilst they graze.

My only experience of coolie transport was from Tokhan to Zimmé, when I hired men from each village to carry my baggage a few miles. This was very unsatisfactory, very expensive, and full of delays. Better than this would be to hire Kamoos (a hardy race inhabiting the northern hills and having many of the characteristics of the Hazaras) by the month at Rs. 8 or Rs. 9. Kamoos may be met in gangs all over the northern and central parts of Siam, and at large places like Zimmé and Muang Nan could be readily engaged. Against all coolie transport is the same objection, that is, the addition of a large number of extra human mouths to feed.

Bullock carts are used in all the southern and eastern parts of Siam, and are an excellent form of transport, care being taken to engage them for the trip and not by the stage. In the northern parts carts are unknown, and there are no tracks broad enough for wheeled traffic.

Siam is singularly destitute of mules and ponies: throughout the land, except actually in Bangkok or Zimmé, it is the rarest thing to see a pony of any sort, and then only wretched weedy little rats about twelve hands high, who pick up a precarious living in the gutters. The only places where ponies and mules fit for transport are purchasable are at Bangkok and the large towns on the main trade route between Yunnan and Moulmein, viz. Kiang Hai, Zimmé, Muang Haut, and Rahang—at these latter places only from passing Yunnan or Shan traders. There is no sale for ponies or mules in Siam, and therefore no one breeds them: all, or nearly all, we saw were on their way through to the Moulmein and Rangoon markets.

The traveller who starts from any point in Burmah should certainly buy mules or ponies there for his baggage, unless time is no object and he can afford to saunter along with hired elephants. Against all hired carriage the same objection holds good in Siam, viz. the constant and irritating delays which the traveller is subject to in effecting an exchange of animals. Owners will not as a rule take their animals for more than one or two stages, and at the end of their beat deposit your baggage on the ground and depart (paid or not paid), leaving you to make the best arrangements you can for securing a new set of animals. A traveller may in this way be stranded for weeks in an out-of-the-way village, unable to progress for want of carriage. In fact, the French Consul on his way to Luang Prabang was detained for nearly three months in Zimmé, waiting for elephants: this even though he had orders in writing from the Supreme Government directing that he should be supplied on demand with what carriage he wanted.

It is therefore advisable to be in the matter of carriage entirely independent of the country. I know there are many and almost insuperable disadvantages against an ordinary civilian using mule or pony transport. He may know nothing about their feed and keep; he may be ignorant of the elements of loading pack animals; he may be unable to shoe a pony, unable to prevent sore backs or cure them when made. There is not a shoeing smith or even shoe in the land, out of Bangkok and Zimmé. So that I do not advise the ordinary civilian to dabble in mules or ponies, but the experienced traveller should certainly use them. All horse soldiers and many foot soldiers know enough about this form of transport to get along fast and well with it. In other parts of this book will be found our varied experiences in the transport line; I will not therefore dilate further on the subject, but refer the reader to them, in the hopes he may pick up a few wrinkles useful to him if he follows in our steps.

The traveller by water will find no difficulty in finding suitable boats and prosecuting his journey as far north as Zimmé on the Me Ping River; Muang Phé on the Me Nioum River; Utaradit on the Me Nan River, and Kiangtsen on the Cambodia River. Travelling by this mode can be made most luxurious and comfortable; its drawbacks are the excessive monotony of the journey, and one gets no view of the surrounding country owing to the height of the forest-covered banks; for the most part it is like driving along a very pretty but very monotonous avenue.

The best body servant for a stranger to have in

Siam is a Chinaman who can speak Laos and English. A Chinaman can turn his hands to anything; and if not already a cook, will very soon pick up sufficient of the culinary art to make the traveller fairly comfortable in that respect. In this way it is possible to combine in the person of one man an interpreter, a valet, and a cook. Such a man's pay might be as much as 40 dollars or Rs. 100 a month, but I have heard of good servants being engaged as low as at half that price. It is almost impossible to find a native of the country who knows anything about groom's work, or the keep and feed and loading of pack animals. If possible, therefore, the traveller who intends using mules or ponies should engage Indian Mussulman muleteers in India or Rangoon, and take them on with him.

We had endless trouble in this way, engaging stray Shans to help look after the ponies. They knew nothing about the work, and looked on a pony as a wild and untamable beast. By the time they had learnt a little of their work they got sick of it, and took their discharge. The simplest way is to get mules, fully-equipped drivers and all from Moulmein or Rangoon. If the traveller intends making double marches, as we did all through, his mule loads must not on any account be over 160 lbs., and all long articles, such as tent poles and bed poles, must be eradicated from them.

The Siamese and Laos make very inferior servants, and should only be engaged as a last resource, and used chiefly for foraging, guiding, and interpreting. Better than these is a Madrassi or Mussulman servant. I used to hate Ananias, my Madrassi cook-boy, with an all-abiding hatred very often; but now I come to look back on his performances, I must confess that they were most creditable; and I am afraid Judh Bir and I were rather hard on him for showing the white feather so glaringly when there was any danger. They tell me that even the most martial of Madrassis are not particularly fond of wading about in gore, and therefore we ought not to have expected an overwhelming show of courage in a poor cook-boy.

Travelling by boat one need stint oneself in nothing; with a little forethought and management it is possible to live as comfortably on board a Siamese boat as in one's own mess. The same applies in a lesser degree when employing carts. With pack animals the case is very different, and considerable ingenuity is required in collecting such stores as will furnish the maximum of nourishment with the minimum of weight and bulk. These we found to be—tablets of dried and compressed soup, Canadian tinned beef, cocoa, tea, and whisky; the amount of each being of course calculated according to the amount of carriage available, and the period for which they are intended to last. Living rather low, we found that the above stores lasted one person as follows:—A soup tablet, six days; a tin of beef, four days; a small tin of cocoa, ten days; one lb. of tea, fifteen days; one bottle of whisky, twelve days.

Tents as used in India are unnecessary in Siam, a single sheet of American drill with eyelet holes at the corners being quite sufficient protection from the dew, and the forest trees afford ample shelter from the sun. No tent poles need be carried, bamboos being found everywhere, and are easily cut down and utilized as tent poles. We carried one of these tent d'abris with us, but only pitched it about half-a-dozen times, a large tree or waterproof sheet thrown over a trestle being used instead to keep off the dew. At all villages the traveller will find a welcome and shelter in the guest house which is attached to every village temple.

A camp bed should always be carried, the long

poles having hinges in the middle. A Warren's cooking pot is the best utensil to take if your cook is a Chinaman, or ordinary up-country degchies for an Indian cook. The temperature varies greatly in different parts of Siam. In the north the nights and early mornings, during the winter months, are bitterly cold, and the days bright and just comfortably warm. Further south the greater part of the year is moist and muggy, and the nights even at their coldest only just chilly. Vary though it does, the climate of Siam runs to none of the great extremes to be found in India. The heat is never the heat of the Punjab, and the cold never that of Peshawur in mid-winter. In the way of clothing, therefore, a good even all-round kit will be found most serviceable—not too hot and not too cold. Serge, for instance, is more or less suitable at all seasons. A plentiful supply of boots should be carried, as none are procurable in the country, leather being apparently unused and almost unknown. For bedding three blankets and a waterproof sheet ought to be found sufficient in any part at all seasons. A stout waterproof great-coat should also be taken.

The best months for travelling in Siam, as far

as climate and healthiness are concerned, are the months of January, February, March, and April. During the rains, which last from May to September, land travelling is almost impossible. October, November, and part of December very unhealthy, and malarious fevers are everywhere rife.

All medicines should be carried in the form of gelatinous-covered pills, being more portable and less liable to damage and loss. Quinine, mild aperient and astringent pills for the inner man, and vaseline and iodoform for outside sores and wounds, will be found sufficient medicines for an ordinarily healthy man.